C.H.
and t
Church

Lessons for today from the 'Downgrade' controversy

R. J. Sheehan

___

Grace Publications

GRACE PUBLICATIONS TRUST
139 Grosvenor Avenue,
London, N5 2NH, England.

© R. J. Sheehan 1985

First published 1985

ISBN 0 946462 05 4

Distributed by: EVANGELICAL PRESS,
16/18 High Street, Welwyn,
Herts. AL6 9EQ, England.

Typeset by Inset, Chappel, Essex.
Printed and bound in Great Britain by
Anchor Brendon Ltd, Tiptree, Essex

Contents

Preface

Of necessity any book that seeks to trace an historical controversy will reflect the nature of that controversy. C. H. Spurgeon's attack on the infiltration of modernism into nonconformity led him to separate from the modernists. By its very nature that was a largely negative act and this book is, therefore, largely negative.

The desire of C. H. Spurgeon in separating from modernism was that after separation there might come a greater unity amongst those committed to the evangelical faith. The fact that so few joined him in separation and that he died within a few years of the controversy did not enable him to work out the more positive aspects of evangelical unity. Positive teaching about evangelical unity must, therefore, only be a secondary part of recording this controversy or of applying its lessons to the modern world.

As this book is an historical survey, readers should not expect to find detailed exposition of scripture to justify C. H. Spurgeon's stand. Detailed exegetical argument will have to be presented elsewhere.

Those criticisms which are offered of modern organisations and persons are not the result of spite or animosity but of genuine concern that the lessons of the 'Downgrade' should be understood and applied in the modern situation also.

1

Responsibility for the views expressed is mine alone.

R. J. Sheehan
Welwyn
January 1985

1.
Setting the scene

Charles Haddon Spurgeon was reared amongst Independents, converted under the Methodists and ministered, primarily, among the Baptists. He was in every sense a committed evangelical and nonconformist. He loved the Lord Jesus Christ and the scriptures fervently. He was the leading preacher of the nineteenth century and one of the greatest preachers of all time.

The evangelical churches of Spurgeon's day had a chequered history. After a period of doctrinal unity in a common Calvinistic faith and a time of considerable influence under the Protectorship of Oliver Cromwell, the nonconformists had known much hardship. Virtual disintegration had occurred when their external circumstances became easier. Whereas they had flourished in difficult days, toleration brought decline. As Piette rightly said, "With the prospect of struggles, tortures and hangings gone, life seemed to lose all its zest. For them, religious fervour and persecution were things which went hand in hand. When one ceased, the other likewise disappeared."[1]

The eighteenth century saw not only "the age of reason" in the world in general, but human reason was put at the heart of Christian theology, so that mysterious doctrines such as the Trinity were dismissed as irrational. By the end of the century

hardly a Presbyterian congregation remained that
upheld the deity of the Lord Jesus Christ or which
had much respect for the supernatural in religion at
all. The Congregationalists followed the same slide
downhill (downgrade) as did many General Baptists.
The main thing was to be reasonable and to ignore
revelation.[2]

The only portion of evangelicalism to escape
virtually unscathed by the rationalist onslaught
was the Particular Baptists, although in a sense
they had the same problems. They used their reason
to be scholastic rather than sceptical. Antinomian
and hyper-Calvinistic controversies sapped their
energies and left them orthodox in faith (in general)
but ineffective.

Alongside this obsession with human reason in
the churches there was an increasing scepticism about
traditional views of the Bible in the theological
colleges. The traditional (and biblical) contention
that Moses authored the Pentateuch came under
increasing scrutiny. Initially the suggestion was
made that Moses had used several sources to com-
pile his work. Soon up to forty sources were "dis-
cerned" and some were dated long after Moses in
the exile. The biblical contention that Moses wrote
the Pentateuch was being dismissed, and with it
biblical authority and infallibility were being rejected.
This reassessment of scripture known as "Higher
Criticism" was greatly advanced in the eighteenth
century and became the obsession of German
theology in the nineteenth century.[3]

At the end of the eighteenth and the beginning
of the nineteenth centuries certain things turned the

tide for evangelicalism so that a degree of evangelical orthodoxy was recovered. The Methodist revival gave a measure of impetus to the evangelical cause. Those General Baptists that had remained evangelical separated from the rationalists and formed a new General Baptist connexion. The Particular Baptists shook off hyper-Calvinism (although many Strict Baptists retained it) and threw themselves into missionary work and education for the ministry, to be closely followed and copied by the General Baptists. This new desire to preach the gospel did much to bring new life to evangelicalism.

As both the General Baptists and Particular Baptists engaged in missionary work and the education of ministers, they began to look more closely at each other. Many of the Particular Baptists began to renounce the strict discipline that barred the unbaptised from the Lord's table and began to hold their Calvinism less tightly. The General Baptists were generally opposed to Calvinism and its "narrowness" and open to receive influence from all directions. Many of them wanted to be open, wide, big-hearted evangelicals. This unwillingness to be dogmatic, and willingness to listen to all, opened the door for unorthodox belief once more.

It was in the Baptist Union, founded in 1813, that this breadth of opinion was to find its way and where C. H. Spurgeon would fight and lose his last great battle.

Before that great battle could commence German rationalism had to gain its foothold in England and infiltrate the evangelical constituency. Every part of evangelicalism was subtly infected. Few ministers openly preached in an unorthodox manner. Rather, they began to omit certain truths and then slowly to promote error. C. H. Spurgeon first entered into controversy over a hymn-book. This is the subject of the next chapter.

References

1. Quoted Underwood A. C. (1947) *A History of English Baptists.* Kingsgate Press. p. 117.
2. Ibid. pp. 116—148.
3. For a detailed history of the development of Higher Criticism see Harrison, R. K. (1970) *Introduction to the Old Testament.* Tyndale Press. ch. I—IV.

2.
Early skirmishes

When the Reverend Thomas Toke Lynch published
'The Rivulet' or 'Hymns for the Heart and Voice'
in 1856, those who caustically attacked C. H.
Spurgeon, his creed and his preaching, found much to
praise. They found in the hymnal ideas that would
appeal to those who were "genuine, earnest and
religious" yet who agreed with "the creed of no
church", those who took for their "textbook the
living heart of man rather than the written word".[1]
The terms of such a commendation reveal the reason
for condemnation from evangelical lips. The hymn-
book was obviously a product of natural rather than
scriptural religion.

Mr. James Grant, the editor of the 'Morning
Advertiser', took Mr. Lynch and the newspaper in
which his work had been favourably reviewed ('The
Eclectic Review'), to task. Mr. Grant's attack on
the hymnal was not primarily that it was unorthodox — in that it openly taught error — although he
did assert that there was "an implied denial of the
doctrine of innate and total depravity". Rather
he emphasised its notable omissions: "there was no
distinct recognition of the Divinity of Christ, or of
the mediatorial work and vicarious sacrifice of
the Saviour, or of the personality, office and work
of the Holy Ghost".[2] In fact it was nothing other
than "modified Deism".[3]

Needless to say the Rev. T. T. Lynch replied, supported by a number of notable ministers who vouched for his orthodoxy. But neither Mr. Grant nor his supporters were satisfied.

In May, C. H. Spurgeon entered the fray giving a lengthy review of the hymnal. He asserted his agreement "with the men who have censured the theology of the writer of the hymns".[4] He argued that whatever the poetic merit of the book, it was manifestly unsuitable for a hymnal. It was a work of "talent, mind and research" yet "little calculated to arouse the careless, guide the wanderer, comfort the desponding or edify the believer".[5]

C. H. Spurgeon's conclusions were based on the fact that in the hymnbook there was "nothing distinct . . . but its indistinctness". He asserted that it would be acceptable to the evangelical and unitarian, the lovers and haters of the gospel, because it said nothing clearly.[6] He commended it as a hymnal for Red Indians because "there are some most appropriate sonnets for the worship of the God of nature which the unenlightened savage would understand quite as well as the believer in Revelation and might perhaps receive rather more readily!"[7]

At the close of his review, C. H. Spurgeon asked his readers not to be sidetracked by the consideration of a hymnbook from the real problem in the churches of which the hymnal was a fairly unimportant symptom. The real problem was that unorthodox doctrine was as "seas of latent fire in the bosom of our churches". He continued, "it will, in a few more years, be hard to prove the orthodoxy of our

churches if matters be not changed". The change
that he looked for was that "the day were over when
our churches tamely endure false doctrine". He
concluded with a call to arms "to handle truth not
with kid gloves but with gauntlets . . ." confident
that "the old faith must be triumphant".[8]

The controversy continued for a while with some
force. Some evangelicals were alerted to the dangers
but no real change came about in the churches or
in their tolerance of unorthodox doctrine.

It is necessary to pause and to note how unorthodox doctrine took over many of the evangelical
churches. It was not that error was openly propa-
gated or that truth was denied. Rather it was that
the truths of the scriptures were ignored and replaced
by inoffensive generalities. Men who believed and
taught nothing distinctive or doctrinal were difficult
to condemn for heresy because they were masters
of the indistinct and undefined — men with neither
dogmatism nor conviction, willing to offend none
and listen to all. C. H. Spurgeon well understood
that to hide the truth is as much unorthodoxy as
to deny it. He was as concerned to ask what truths
men omitted as what truths they denied. This lesson
needs to be learned again in the modern setting.

Some four years later C. H. Spurgeon again joined
others in protesting against unorthodoxy. The Rev.
J. Baldwin Brown published a series of sermons
under the title "Divine Life in Man". Many things
were objectionable in the book, not least its favour-
able attitude towards the rejection of substitutionary
atonement and its promotion of unorthodox theological writers and teachers.

In a sermon preached in April 1860, C. H. Spurgeon
attacked the sort of theology found in J. B. Brown's
book and similar publications:

"We have lived to see a certain sort of men . . .
who seek to teach, nowadays, that God is a universal
Father, and that our ideas of His dealing with the
impenitent as a Judge, and not as a Father, are
remnants of antiquated error. Sin, according to
these men, is a disorder rather than an offence,
an error rather than a crime. Love is the only
attribute they can discern, and the full-orbed Deity
they have not known. Some of these men push their
way very far into the bogs and mire of falsehood,
until they inform us that eternal punishment is
ridiculed as a dream. In fact, books now appear
which teach us that there is no such thing as the
vicarious sacrifice of our Lord Jesus Christ. They
use the word atonement, it is true: but, in regard
to its meaning they have removed the ancient land-
mark. They acknowledge that the Father has shown
His great love to poor sinful man by sending His
Son, but not that God was inflexibly just in the
exhibition of His mercy, nor that he punished Christ
on behalf of His people, nor that, indeed, God ever
will punish anybody in His wrath, or that there is
such a thing as justice apart from discipline. Even
sin and hell are but old words employed henceforth in a new and altered sense . . . These are the
new men whom God has sent down from Heaven to
tell us that the apostle Paul was all wrong, that our
faith is vain, that we have been quite mistaken, and
that there was no need for propitiating blood to wash
away our sins: that the fact was, our sins needed

discipline, but penal vengeance and righteous wrath are quite out of the question! When I thus speak, I am free to confess that such ideas are not boldly taught by a certain individual whose volume excites these remarks, but as he puffs the books of gross perverters of the truth, I am compelled to believe that he endorses such theology."[9]

C. H. Spurgeon's last sentence again shows the difficulty that the evangelicals had with the evasive tactics of the unorthodox. Error was not so much spelt out as implied. Pointers were given that led away from biblical truth. The new theology with its rationalism was advocated and praised. But others than C. H. Spurgeon could see where this was leading. The Unitarians promised sympathy and prayer to the new thinkers who were moving in their direction.[10]

J. H. Hinton first attacked J. B. Brown's book because he saw it as the first major literary work in favour of unorthodox doctrine among evangelicals. He wrote, "I speak because I would fain contribute somewhat, however little, to withstand what I take to be the first open inroad, into English Evangelical Nonconformist churches, of a theology fatally deficient in the truth and power of the Gospel."[11] Because C. H. Spurgeon agreed, he supported J. H. Hinton by word and pen.

Replies were received from various of J. B. Brown's colleagues and supporters but none is more interesting than his own. He wrote, "I content myself with declaring, in the belief that there are men in the Baptist ministry candid enough to find my words credible, that the doctrines of grace, in the broad, full, Evangelic sense of the term, have for nearly twenty years been the great theme of my ministry and, if I know my own heart, will be till I die."[12]

The cleverness of the reply cannot but be noticed. J. B. Brown knew that he did not hold to the doctrines of grace in the commonly understood sense but reinterpreted and perverted them. He affirmed his belief in them in the "broad full, Evangelic sense". Using the principles of elasticity and remoulding, he used evangelical terms for unorthodox beliefs. C. H. Spurgeon and others knew that correct terminology was not enough. Clear definition was also needed. But J. B. Brown knew that many Baptists would be happy as long as he used the correct terms and assured them he was evangelical.

The subsequent history of the church and the modern situation demonstrate that the methods of the non-evangelical have not changed. Modern theology loves to quote the scriptures, the Reformers and the Creeds, but puts totally new meanings into the terms used, knowing that most Christians are gullible enough to accept anything that sounds evangelical even if it is heretical.

In putting his name to a letter of which Joseph Angus was the author, C. H. Spurgeon recognised that modern theologians would attack him and his associates as being anti-intellectual and old-fashioned. But by this the signatories were not moved. In his 15th April 1860 sermon, C. H. Spurgeon commented on J. B. Brown's book:

"Well, brethren, I am happy to say that sort of stuff has not gained entrance into this pulpit. I dare say the worms will eat the wood before there will be anything of that sort sounded in this place; and may these bones be picked by vultures, and this flesh be rent in sunder by lions, and may every nerve in this body suffer pangs and tortures, ere these lips shall give utterance to any such doctrines or sentiments! We are content to remain among the vulgar souls who believe the old doctrines of grace. We are willing still to be behind in the great march of intellect, and stand by that unmoving cross, which, like the pole star, never advances, because it never stirs, but always abides in its place, the guide of the soul to heaven, the one foundation other than which no man can lay, and without building upon which no man shall ever see the face of God and live."[13]

In the years that followed, the situation steadily worsened. Higher Criticism and modernistic theology came in stealthily and then openly through Anglicans such as Bishop Colenso of Natal and T. K. Cheyne, through Presbyterians such as A. B. Davidson, through Congregationalists such as R. W. Dale. Some of the most prominent preachers valued Higher Criticism and taught evangelicalism. The more they accepted the former, the less they were committed to the latter. Just a few years before the 'Downgrade' controversy broke, Julius Wellhausen, the 'father' of Higher Criticism, published his theory by which he not only named the sources behind the Pentateuch but imposed evolutionary theory on the Old Testament with the result that the whole of Old Testament theology was drastically reconstructed.

The new criticism was about to take England by storm, so that after the publication of S. R. Driver's 'Introduction to the Literature of the Old Testament' in 1891, "A close if unofficial surveillance was imposed upon potential candidates for positions in the Old Testament field in British universities, and only those who displayed proper respect for the canons of critical orthodoxy were appointed to academic posts. Consequently, scholars of a more conservative bent were relegated to comparative obscurity in theological colleges of various denominations and other independent institutions of learning."[14]

The scene was set for the 'Downgrade' controversy. Generally, commitment to Calvinism among the Baptists was in decline, the "broad" view of doctrinal belief and statement was well in the ascendancy, toleration was applauded, dogmatism and conviction were deplored and the great decline of English evangelicalism was being ushered in by those who used evangelical language to propagate unorthodoxy, who ignored biblical doctrines and taught trite, rationalistic sentimentalities in their place.

References
1.   See *The Early Years,* Spurgeon's Autobiography Vol. I (1962). Banner of Truth pp. 471–472.
2.   ibid. p. 472.
3.   ibid. p. 473.
4.   ibid. p. 474.
5.   ibid. p. 477.
6.   ibid. p. 477.
7.   ibid. p. 478.
8.   ibid. pp. 480–481.
9.   ibid. p. 488.
10. ibid. p. 495.
11. ibid. p. 482.
12. ibid. p. 494.
13. ibid. pp. 488–489.
14. Harrison, R. K. op. cit. p. 28.

3.
Opening the wound

C. H. Spurgeon's monthly magazine 'The Sword and Trowel' became the literary organ through which the battles of the 'Downgrade' controversy were waged. The contents were prepared for the press two weeks before publication and this fact needs to be borne in mind in tracing the development of the controversy.

The January 1887 edition of 'The Sword and Trowel' opened the attack in a very indirect way. Joseph Cook reviewed the history of rationalism in Germany in an article 'Decline of Rationalism in German Universities'.[1] He stated that, whereas at the beginning of the eighteenth century the students had deserted the evangelical lectures for the rationalists, eighty years of speculation from the rationalists had reduced their number of students to less than a dozen in most of their faculties whereas the evangelicals lectured to hundreds.

C. H. Spurgeon concluded this article with a note in parenthesis. It was sarcastic and cutting, yet ironically true. He wrote, "We have inserted this paragraph for the special delight of those 'advanced brethren' who have of late so sagely picked up what the Germans have thrown away. By the time they have got the old Teutonic small-clothes comfortably fitted upon themselves, the Germans will all have become orthodox; and then our learned brothers will have to strip again, and get into the new fashion just as it is waxing old. Very funny these twistings of the infallibly wise! Very wicked of these Farderlanders to lead our witless sophists into ditches, and then leave them there!"[2]

The biting sarcasm of C. H. Spurgeon was not likely to endear him to others; especially not in the climate of the 1880's among Baptists where the union of the General and Particular Baptists was a great hope. C. H. Spurgeon's attack on the modernists would be counterproductive to such union, which required a papering over of distinctions for the sake of unity. Prominent among those calling for unity amongst the different branches of the Baptists was Charles Williams. In 1886 he called for fusion and this was put to the churches in 1887 and found general enthusiasm. John Clifford also pressed for union as he considered the Calvinistic hindrance virtually dead.[3]

Both Charles Williams and John Clifford had rejected the doctrine of inerrancy and were prized for their breadth of heart.[4] John Clifford was praised by W. E. Blomfeld (who had been investigated for heresy) for his "broad interpretation of Evangelicalism, his appreciation of the work of Biblical scholarship, his resolute opposition to blind conservatism, his repudiation of the antagonism between Religion and Science so often proclaimed by some in our own church".[5] He was Vice President of the Baptist Union in 1887.

As Charles Williams and John Clifford called for Baptist unity and broad, Arminian, scholastic evangelicalism, C. H. Spurgeon gave a brief, but pointed, response in the February 'Sword and Trowel':

"Constantly we hear of proposals for union, and
truly these are welcome where mere technical matters
divide true Christians; but what is the use of pretend-
ing to create union where there can be none? There
is another matter which needs to be thought of as
well as union, and that is TRUTH. To part with
truth to show charity is to betray our Lord with a
kiss. Between those who believe in the eternal verities
and those who constantly cast doubt on them there
can be no union. One cried of old, 'Is it peace?' And
the answer was a sharp and true one. We render it
thus — 'What hast thou to do with peace while
departures from the truth of God are so many?'
The first question is — Are we one in Christ? and
are we obedient to the truth revealed in the Scriptures? If so, union will necessarily follow: but if not,
it is vain to clamour for a confederacy which would
only be an agreement to aid and abet each other's
errors."[6]

We need to notice that C. H. Spurgeon saw expres-
sions of the unity of true Christians as desirable. He
was not an isolationist. He wanted unity with Christ-
loving, Bible-believing brethren. But he wanted such
unity without giving signs of fellowship and acceptance to those who attacked the truths and truthfulness of scripture. Love did not require alliance with
error.

The brief notes of January and February were
followed in March by the article from which the
controversy received its name. Many assumed that
the article was the work of C. H. Spurgeon. In fact,
it was written by Robert Shindler and published by
C. H. Spurgeon, with an interesting footnote. The

article was called 'The Downgrade' and Mr. Spurgeon's footnote stated, "Earnest attention is requested for this paper. There is need of such a warning as this history affords. We are going downhill at break-neck speed."[7]

In this first article on the 'Downgrade', Robert Shindler traced the rapid decline into Arianism and Socinianism of the nonconformist churches (this was noted in our first chapter concerning the eighteenth century) in the following statement: "By some means or other, first the ministers, and then the churches, got on the 'down-grade', and in some cases the descent was rapid, and in all, disastrous."[8]

Robert Shindler traced this decline and its reasons. They may be listed as follows:

1. A rejection of Puritan piety and Calvinistic doctrine for less simple, more speculative moral teaching and natural theology. "Sermons became more and more Christless."[9]

2. More attention was paid to learning, scholarship and oratory than to godliness, orthodoxy and evangelical zeal. Even where orthodoxy was retained it became cold and formal and speculative in a hyper-Calvinist way.

3. The language of orthodoxy was retained but its concepts were redefined and only gradually brought out in the teaching.

4. The orthodox allowed the unorthodox into their pulpits and had them as assistants and even successors.

5. No credal test was used to determine who should preach or commune or whatever.

These five reasons were stated by Mr. Shindler as at the heart of evangelical decline in the eighteenth century. No Baptist reading the 'Sword and Trowel' could have failed to draw parallels with the situation in the 1880's. The leading Baptists who desired union were anti-Calvinists, infatuated with Higher Criticism, fraternising with and defending sentiments, and their propagators, contrary to the evangelical faith. The great insistence of those most keen on Baptist unity was that there must be no credal test.[10]

In the April 'Sword and Trowel' C. H. Spurgeon gave his colleagues a lot of space to argue the case one way and the other. A short unsigned article by 'an old divine' set out six trials of sincerity to test hypocrites and concluded that "This is an age of false doctrine in the pulpit, and hollow profession in the pew; do not trust either thyself or any other man, but try the spirits, both thine own and the preachers."[11]

This was followed by Robert Shindler's second article 'The Down Grade'[12], to which C. H. Spurgeon added the footnote, "Again we call special attention to this most important theme. The growing evil demands the attention of all who desire the prosperity of the church of God."

In his article, Mr. Shindler traced the down grade in the established church where men of high learning, eloquence and abilities introduced Arian and Socinian heresies. He then turned to the Independents and General Baptists. Again we may list his main contentions.

1. Error prevailed because people were impressed by learning and oratory, not orthodoxy.

2. Error prevailed because orthodox ministers exchanged pulpits and fraternised with the unorthodox, thus lessening the suspicion of the people towards unorthodoxy.

3. Theological training became undogmatic, discussing the virtues of orthodoxy and unorthodoxy and allowing lecturers to hold either set of views.

4. Only where modern thought has been fiercely fought has orthodoxy revived and prevailed.

5. "The first step astray is a want of adequate faith in the divine inspiration of the sacred Scriptures. All the while a man bows to the authority of God's Word, he will not entertain any sentiment contrary to its teaching . . . But let a man question, or entertain low views of the inspiration and authority of the Bible, and he is without chart to guide him and without anchor to hold him . . . In looking carefully over the history of the times, and the movement of the times, of which we have briefly written, this fact is apparent, that where ministers and Christian churches have held fast to the truth that the Holy Scriptures have been given by God as an authoritative and infallible rule of faith and practice they have never wandered seriously out of the way. But when, on the other hand, reason has been exalted above revelation, and made the exponent of revelation, all kinds of errors and mischiefs have been the result."[13]

6. That Calvinists generally leave the scriptures last of all.

7. Rationalism empties churches. The gospel maintains them.

C. H. Spurgeon as editor of 'The Sword and

Trowel' then included an article on 'Ministerial
Reserve' by James Dann,[14] in which two sets of
ministers were attacked: (i) those who were unorthodox in doctrine but were fearful of openly
joining the unorthodox and so stayed in the churches
and undermined the faith, and (ii) those who were
evangelical in doctrine but were frightened of being
thought old-fashioned and unscholarly by the unorthodox and who would not speak up and out
for evangelicalism. James Dann attacked these
"brethren of the Yea-and-Nay order" and called
them to be manly, to stand up and be counted. No
reader of the article could feel comfortable as a
neutral. Compromise was roundly condemned.

Following this C. H. Spurgeon printed an article
confirming the earlier article of Joseph Cook in
which T. Witton Davies argued that the rationalist
teachers had failed miserably in Germany, Holland
and France and that they were being discarded for
evangelical teachers. The churches which rationalism
had emptied were being filled by evangelical
ministers.

At the end of the April edition, C. H. Spurgeon
added his comments: "We are glad that the article
upon 'The Down Grade' has excited notice. It is
not intended to be an attack on anyone but to be
a warning to all."[15]

Some of his readers had seen the attack as an
attack from a Calvinist on Arminianism. C. H.
Spurgeon rejected this. He accepted that historic-
ally Arminianism had been the usual way to
Socinianism but stated, "We care far more for the
central evangelical truths than we do for Calvinism

as a system; but we believe that Calvinism has in it
a conservative force which helps to hold men to
vital truth, and therefore we are sorry to see any
quitting it who once accepted it. Those who hold
the eternal verities of salvation, and yet do not see
all that we believe and embrace, are by no means
the objects of our opposition; our warfare is with
men who are giving up the atoning sacrifice, denying
the inspiration of Holy Scripture and casting slurs
upon justification by faith. The present struggle is
not a debate upon the question of Calvinism or
Arminianism but of the truth of God versus the
invention of men. All who believe the gospel should
unite against that 'modern thought' which is its
deadly enemy".[16]

Again C. H. Spurgeon was attacked for hindering
unity and lacking love. He replied, "On all hands
we hear cries for unity in this and unity in that; but
to our mind the main need of this age is not compromise but conscientiousness. 'First pure, then
peaceable'. It is easy to cry 'A confederacy', but
that union which is not based on the truth of God
is rather a conspiracy than a communion. Charity
by all means: but honesty also. Love, of course, but
love to God as well as love to men, and love of truth
as well as love of union. It is exceedingly difficult
in these times to preserve one's fidelity before God
and one's fraternity among men. Should not the
former be preferred to the latter if both cannot be
maintained? We think so."[17]

By the end of the April issue of 'The Sword and
Trowel', C. H. Spurgeon and his colleagues had
opened the wound. The attack had been made. The

churches had been warned. Having shown how
unorthodoxy spreads, C. H. Spurgeon gave his friends
opportunity to show how unorthodoxy should be
stemmed.

References
1. 'Sword and Trowel' January 1887 p. 18.
2. ibid. p. 18.
3. Underwood op. cit. pp. 215, 216.
4. ibid. p. 230.
5. ibid. p. 226.
6. 'Sword and Trowel' February 1887 p. 91.
7. 'Sword and Trowel' March 1887 pp. 122—126.
8. ibid. p. 122.
9. ibid. p. 122.
10. Underwood op. cit. pp. 215, 216.
11. 'Sword and Trowel' April 1887 p. 165.
12. ibid. pp. 166—172.
13. ibid. p. 170.
14. ibid. pp. 172—174.
15. ibid. p. 195.
16. ibid. pp. 195—196.
17. ibid. p. 196.

4.
'The struggle needful to deliver our churches'

C. H. Spurgeon and his colleagues had called on all those who upheld the inspiration and authority of the scriptures and who loved the gospel to stand together openly and fearlessly against those who attacked the scriptures and distorted the gospel.

He and his colleagues had given indications how this battle was to be waged. They had called for the clear and zealous preaching of the gospel, the uncompromising teaching of the old truths, the rejection of alliances of any sort with opponents of the scriptures and the gospel, and for utter honesty and clarity in what was said. They had called men from positions of neutrality and indecision to stand for truth and against error. In the pulpits, the colleges and in the alliances that were created, unity in the truth had to be seen and heard.

When handed a paper on John Stanger of Bessels Green, C. H. Spurgeon decided to print it, although it was lengthy, as "a fine illustration of what is meant by the 'Downgrade' and of the struggle needful to deliver our churches from it".[1] The author saw the life of John Stanger as illustrating the "tendency of unevangelical sentiments towards religious deadness and heresy" and "the upward and expansive potency of sound views of Divine truth".[2] Again we may list the points made:

1. That the decline from evangelical truth began

not by a willing rejection of it, but by defective views of the depravity of man and of salvation by grace on the part of sincere Arminians. The more general their views of salvation became the more they declined.

2. John Stanger began attacking Arianism and Socinianism as the assistant to an Arian, Socinian General Baptist minister. He attacked these views by preaching "the three R's — Ruin, Redemption, Regeneration".[3] He did not seek controversy but preached truth. "I thought it my incumbent duty to be more express in regard to those doctrines which constitute the peculiar glory of the Gospel such as the personal dignity of Jesus Christ, the sufficiency of his obedience and death to save, justification by faith only, the depravity of human nature, and the necessity and reality of the Holy Spirit's influence."[4]

3. John Stanger continued to teach truths in spite of much opposition and refused to give way to his opponents. The church ultimately split. Stanger's church remained and grew. The old heretical church died out. John Stanger opened ten additional chapels for preaching.

Nothing more was mentioned in the May issue of 'The Sword and Trowel'. By including the article C. H. Spurgeon had encouraged his Baptist brethren to tenaciously preach the old Calvinistic gospel with vigour and fullness and to win through whatever the cost — even if it split churches.

The exact date at which the Secretary of the Baptist Union, Dr. S. H. Booth, wrote to C. H. Spurgeon is not known, but about this time letters were sent. In them Dr. Booth expressed his concern at the public statements of some of the Baptist Union Council and at the tendency of the teaching of the Baptist Colleges. Knowing that there was no machinery existing in the Baptist Union to deal with such heresy, he asked C. H. Spurgeon to act and supplied him with the names of offenders and the speeches which caused offence.

This intervention by Dr. Booth was most significant. It is not now clear what Dr. Booth expected C. H. Spurgeon to do. A review of the teaching given in 'The Sword and Trowel' up to this point in time suggests that C. H. Spurgeon was calling for:

1. The open rejection of unorthodoxy by evangelicals.
2. The clear proclamation of evangelicalism in the pulpits and the colleges.
3. The rejection of proposals for union with the unorthodox.
4. The unity of evangelicals.
5. The refusal by evangelicals to share their pulpits with the unorthodox.
6. A credal requirement for fellowship.

A survey of these six points will make it clear that a man like Dr. Booth may well have understood C. H. Spurgeon to be saying that the time had come to make no more concessions to the unorthodox. Concessions had gone far enough. Dr. Booth was happy to encourage C. H. Spurgeon to take the lead in calling a halt to these concessions — especially once C. H. Spurgeon made it clear that he was not insisting on a return to Calvinism, although he would have preferred that to happen.

It must also be noticed that C. H. Spurgeon expressed himself in terms that suggested that unorthodoxy was looming as a threat to which Baptists were moving and not that it was in control already. Baptists were "going downhill"[5] but had not arrived at the bottom. Unorthodoxy was a "growing evil"[6] but had not yet prevailed. Many Baptists like Dr. Booth wrote to C. H. Spurgeon and looked for a lead in preventing further decline but as events were to prove they never intended him, nor were they themselves willing, to deal in a disciplinary manner with the men and churches who were spreading unorthodoxy. They were willing to see unorthodoxy checked but not to see it excluded.

In republishing the life of John Stanger, C. H. Spurgeon may well have created a wrong impression about his intentions. John Stanger stayed in an unorthodox denomination as assistant to a heretical pastor until forced to accept division by a split in the church. Ultimately he prevailed and unorthodoxy faltered. Dr. Booth may well have understood C. H. Spurgeon to be advocating a policy of remaining in the denomination until he was deposed or prevailed — what in the modern world is called an "in it to win it" policy, holding on to the truth and proclaiming it until it triumphs over unorthodoxy. Dr. Booth may have seen C. H. Spurgeon as the focal point for such a group among the Baptists.

In his footnote to the article on John Stanger, C. H. Spurgeon, however, had not commended Stanger's strategy, only his tenacity. He rejoiced to read of a man who preached truth and upheld it in the face of error. The writer of the article also used

Stanger as an illustration of how truth causes
churches to flourish and error destroys them. He
did not suggest that Stanger had necessarily always
acted correctly.

In the June edition of 'The Sword and Trowel',
Robert Shindler gave an account of the trial of five
professors of the Congregational College of Andover,
Massachusetts for heresy.[7] The issue was whether
they were teaching what the founders of the College
intended them to teach as laid down in the doctrinal
statement of the College.

The professors argued that they were "pro-
gressively orthodox".[8] Robert Shindler was merciless
in his exposure of the meaning of this phrase. "The
progressiveness of the professors seems to be like
that of the preacher whose two divisions of his subject were: 'First, my brethren, I shall go round the
text; and secondly, my friends, I shall go right away
from it'. Indeed the progression is so considerable
that the 'orthodoxy' is lost sight of."[9]

Mr. Shindler then proceeded to show how the
Andover professors had unorthodox views of the
inspiration and authority of scripture, the Person
of Christ, union with Christ, depravity, and second
probation, and demonstrated how essential these
were to the evangelical faith.

In concluding, he affirmed the need to stand
together for evangelicalism with evangelical
Arminians who were sound in their doctrine of
scripture and committed to the atoning work of
Christ. He called on the readers to give place to
"progressive orthodoxy" "no, not for an hour".[10]

The silence of the July edition of 'The Sword and

Trowel' on the whole matter might have encouraged
the unorthodox to think that the magazine and its
editor had finished with the issue. A call to stand
for evangelicalism had been given. Now it would be
left.

The silent month was, in fact, very significant.
From January to June C. H. Spurgeon had limited
himself to notes and footnotes. Joseph Cook, James
Dann, T. Witton Davies and, most notably, Robert
Shindler had written all the articles. C. H. Spurgeon
had determined to respond to Dr. Booth and his
other correspondents and to enter the fray personally. The first article in the August edition of 'The
Sword and Trowel' was from his pen.

References
1.   'The Sword and Trowel' May 1887 pp. 230—238.
2.   ibid. p. 230.
3.   ibid. p. 235.
4.   ibid. p. 235.
5.   'The Sword and Trowel' March 1887 p. 122.
6.   'The Sword and Trowel' April 1887 p. 166.
7.   'The Sword and Trowel' June 1887 pp. 274—280.
8.   ibid. p. 274.
9.   ibid. p. 274.
10.   ibid. p. 280.

5.
Into the fray

In the opening article of the August edition of 'The Sword and Trowel',[1] C. H. Spurgeon expressed his concern in no uncertain terms. He began his attack with a reference to the nonconformist newspapers that favoured unorthodoxy. "Read those newspapers which represent the Broad School of Dissent and ask yourself, How much farther could they go? What doctrine remains to be abandoned? What other truth to be the object of contempt? A new religion has been initiated which is no more Christianity than chalk is cheese."[2]

He then attacked the dishonesty of the new 'orthodoxy'. It claimed to be no more than the old orthodoxy "with slight improvements" and using this as its plea happily preached in churches established for the gospel.[3]

C. H. Spurgeon then listed the 'improvements'. "The atonement is scouted, the inspiration of Scripture is derided, the Holy Spirit is degraded into an influence, the punishment of sin is turned into fiction and the resurrection into a myth, and yet these enemies of our faith expect us to call them brethren, and maintain a confederacy with them".[4] The strong language of enmity and the rejection of an alliance with the unorthodox set the whole tone of the article and the events following it. The key word is 'maintain'. Here C. H. Spurgeon revealed the fact that he viewed himself in alliance with enemies of the gospel and sowed the seed of his imminent separation from them. Whereas others among the Baptists wanted to stop the advance of unorthodoxy but were happy to maintain the *status quo,* C. H. Spurgeon questioned whether remaining in alliance with such men was desirable.

As in previous articles by his colleagues, C. H. Spurgeon pointed out that doctrinal decline had led to a lessening of commitment to devotional life, e.g. prayer meetings, and an increasing commitment to the world, e.g. attendance at theatres. He tersely summarised it, "The fact is, that many would like to unite church and stage, cards and prayer, dancing and sacraments."[5]

He expressed his fear that history was about to repeat itself: that the decline from Puritan evangelicalism and godliness into unitarianism in the seventeenth and eighteenth centuries was to be copied by a decline from the evangelical revival of the eighteenth century through ministers "toying with the deadly cobra of 'another gospel' in the form of 'modern thought'".[6]

He noted the departure of many godly people from nonconformity to the Christian Brethren and the Anglicans. He saw nonconformity in rapid decline because the gospel and prayer were being slighted.

With particular vehemence C. H. Spurgeon turned on the ministers who made men unbelievers by their unorthodox teaching and sneers. "Avowed atheists are not a tenth as dangerous as those preachers who scatter doubt and stab at faith".[7] He noticed how, after the initial interest created by their new ideas had passed, their chapels emptied and they consoled themselves that this was due to lack of intellect among their hearers! "These destroyers of our churches appear to be as content with their work as monkeys with their mischief. That which our fathers would have lamented they rejoice in: the alienation of the poor and simple minded from their ministry they accept as a compliment and the grief of the spiritually minded they regard as an evidence of their power."[8]

With unconverted, unorthodox ministers increasingly causing trouble in the churches, C. H. Spurgeon declared his determination to act as a watchdog in the presence of burglars by plain speaking.

In his two final paragraphs, C. H. Spurgeon set the scene for the battle ahead. He wrote, "It now becomes a serious question how far those who abide by the faith once delivered to the saints should fraternise with those who have turned aside to another gospel. Christian love has its claims, and divisions are to be shunned as grievous evils; but how far are we justified in being in confederacy with those who are departing from the truth?"[9] He noted the tendency to put denominational unity above truth and to accept anything as long as the person who said it was "a clever man and a good natured brother".[10]

C. H. Spurgeon concluded, "We fear it is hopeless ever to form a society which can keep out men base enough to profess one thing and believe another; but it might be possible to make an informal alliance among all who hold the Christianity of their fathers. Little as they might be able to do, they could at least protest, and as far as possible free themselves of that complicity which will be involved in a conspiracy of silence. If for a while the evangelicals are doomed to go down, let them die fighting, and in the full assurance that their gospel will have a resurrection when the inventions of 'modern thought' shall be burned up with fire unquenchable."[11]

The two great questions were asked:

1. Was it not time to cease alliances with heretics?
2. Was it not time to unite with all who loved the old faith against heresy?

The unity that C. H. Spurgeon envisaged was not an organisational one. It was an 'informal alliance':[12] a commitment of ministers and churches to each other not because they agreed on everything but because they agreed on the great centralities of the faith, and agreed in their rejection of error and alliance with its propagators.

Later in the same issue C. H. Spurgeon made a few comments on "Rationalism in the Established Church"[13] by commenting on the publication of a book disseminating the theories of the father of Higher Criticism,[14] Julius Wellhausen. C. H. Spurgeon hoped that the absurdity of his teachings would be their own antidote as they were "calculated only to befool those who are ignorant".[15] In so hoping he lamentably underestimated the effect of those ideas on an unorthodox 'scholarly' world.

C. H. Spurgeon opened the September edition of 'The Sword and Trowel' with "Our Reply to Sundry Critics and Enquirers".[16] He affirmed that his

post-bag confirmed and multiplied his worst fears
about the state of evangelicalism and the infringe-
ments of unorthodoxy. He noted that no one had
refuted him with any hard evidence. He restated his
conviction that he was not contending upon minor
matters but on matters vital to religion. "Others
may trifle about such things; we cannot and dare
not".[17] He noted that his opponents sought to
ignore his attacks on unorthodoxy by suggesting
his illness (gout) had made him irritable! He repudiated this charge as insolent, untrue and evasive.

He thanked the periodical 'Word and Work' for
supporting him and confirming his contentions. He
quoted it as in support of the idea that the time had
come to speak out and expose error in spite of the
fact that unorthodoxy alone was in fashion and
received praise.

He further refuted the allegation that he had
written rashly and with little evidence. He lamented
his reticence in not writing before but he had held
back to preserve unity. He rejected the charge of
being a pessimist as he was confident in the triumph
of the cause of God ultimately. "Bad as things are
from one point of view, there is a bright side to
affairs: the Lord has yet his men in reserve who
have not bowed the knee to Baal".[18]

He then quoted from other letters that showed
the influence of unorthodoxy was very great not
just in the ministers but in the congregations. He
berated those who were evangelical yet who failed
to speak out. "Are the sceptics so much to the fore
that no man will open his mouth against them? Are
all the orthodox afraid · of the ridicule of the

'cultured'? . . . Christian people are now so tame that they shrink from expressing themselves."[19]

He again explained the real nature of the problem. "A chasm is opening between the men who believe their Bibles and the men who are prepared for an advance upon Scripture. Inspiration and speculation cannot long abide in peace. Compromise there can be none. We cannot hold the inspiration of the Word and yet reject it; we cannot believe in the atonement and deny it; we cannot hold the doctrine of the fall and yet talk of the evolution of spiritual life from human nature; we cannot recognise the punishment of the impenitent and yet indulge the 'larger hope'. One way or the other we must go. Decision is the virtue of the hour."[20]

Having declared the impossibility of holding both truth and error, evangelicalism and unorthodoxy, C. H. Spurgeon concluded, "Neither when we have chosen our way can we keep company with those who go the other way. There must come with decision for truth a corresponding protest against error."[21] He then called on those who agreed with him to wait upon the Lord to determine the next step.

In this last paragraph C. H. Spurgeon articulated what he had implied on many previous occasions: as truth and error are irreconcilable, the evangelical and the unorthodox must walk separate paths. Separation from error and errorists is necessary.

Later in the same issue C. H. Spurgeon exonerated certain congregations from wilfully conniving at unorthodoxy because their trustees had imposed unorthodox men on them against their wishes. He warned other congregations of this danger.[22]

In the notes with which the magazine concluded, C. H. Spurgeon gave notice of the publication of his article on the 'Downgrade' and encouraged its wide circulation "as silence is the favourite policy of the adversary".[23]

After thanking 'The Baptist' newspaper for its "friendly feeling at all times"[24] towards him, C. H. Spurgeon noted that certain denominations proposed not to build chapels to rival each other in the same towns or villages. With this proposal C. H. Spurgeon heartily concurred "where the gospel is truly preached"[25] in the town or village, but where the gospel was not preached he urged the rejection of the proposal because of the duty of preaching the gospel to all. To him the mere existence of a chapel was not enough to prevent rival work. What mattered was what was preached in the chapel!

References

1. 'The Sword and Trowel' August 1887 pp. 397–400.
2. ibid. p. 397.
3. ibid. p. 397.
4. ibid. p. 397.
5. ibid. p. 398.
6. ibid. p. 398.
7. ibid. p. 399.
8. ibid. pp. 399–400.
9. ibid. p. 400.
10. ibid. p. 400.
11. ibid. p. 400.
12. ibid. p. 400.
13. ibid. p. 430.
14. see chapter one.
15. 'The Sword and Trowel' August 1887 p. 430.
16. 'The Sword and Trowel' September 1887 pp. 461–465.
17. ibid. p. 461.
18. ibid. p. 464.
19. ibid. pp. 464–5.
20. ibid. p. 465.
21. ibid. p. 465.
22. ibid. p. 492.
23. ibid. p. 503.
24. ibid. p. 503.
25. ibid. p. 503.

6.
Separation

When Dr. Booth had asked C. H. Spurgeon to do
something about the advance of unorthodoxy he
had not anticipated such a forthright campaign. He
had looked for a stunting of the growth of unorthodoxy but had not dreamed (so subsequent
events suggest) that C. H. Spurgeon would call for
an alliance in the truth and separation from error.

Dr. Booth and a number of other Baptists must
have nervously awaited the October edition of 'The
Sword and Trowel' as October was the month for the
autumn meetings of the Baptist Union in Sheffield.

In his opening article, C. H. Spurgeon wrote of
"The Case Proved".[1] He stated his amazement
that a "company of esteemed friends" had rushed
between him and the unorthodox to say that there
was no reason for contention as there was little
unorthodoxy in nonconformity.[2]

He attributed this concern to reject the charge of
rampant unorthodoxy to the sort of convenient
blindness associated with Nelson by which men,
and particularly denominational officials, feel it
their duty to keep unity at all costs. They see what
they want to see and ignore what is inconvenient
so as to avoid trouble. C. H. Spurgeon wrote, "Either
we are dreaming or our brethren are; let the godly
judge who it is that is asleep".[3]

Drawing from the information that he had collated,

C. H. Spurgeon quoted from the July circular of the
Evangelical Alliance, the report of the Gloucestershire
and Herefordshire Baptist Association and Principal
David Brown of the Free Church College. Each of
these confirmed C. H. Spurgeon's contentions. They
saw the same errors and their consequences.

In his usual masterly manner C. H. Spurgeon
then quoted from two of the leading newspapers
that opposed his theology and promoted unorthodoxy. They recognised the significance of his
statements. The 'Christian World' wrote: "We are
now at the parting of the ways, and the younger
ministers especially must decide whether or not
they will embrace and undisguisedly proclaim that
'modern thought' which in Mr. Spurgeon's eyes is
a 'deadly cobra' while in ours it is the glory of the
century. It discards many of the doctrines dear to
Mr. Spurgeon and his school, not only as untrue
and unscriptural, but as in the strictest sense immoral;
for it cannot recognise the moral possibility of
imputing either guilt or goodness, or the justice of
inflicting everlasting punishment for temporary sin.
It is not so irrational as to pin its faith to verbal
inspiration or so idolatrous as to make its acceptance
of a true Trinity of divine manifestation cover poly-
theism."[4]

This remarkable statement proved C. H. Spurgeon's
claim beyond doubt. This unorthodox newspaper
recognised that men held the doctrines in disguise.
It acclaimed modern thought. It rejected the atonement, imputation, hell, verbal inspiration and the
Trinity and called on ministers to do openly what
they had been doing secretly. "The parting of the
ways" had indeed come.

As the paper had included supportive letters from various ministers, including some Baptists, C. H. Spurgeon asked a question which he emphasised by italics: *"Are brethren who remain orthodox to endorse such sentiments by remaining in union with those who hold and teach them?"*[5]

He continued: "Those gentlemen have full liberty to think as they like; but, on the other hand, those who love the old gospel have equally the liberty to disassociate themselves from them, and that liberty also involves a responsibility from which there is no escaping. If we do not believe in universalism, or in Purgatory, and if we do believe in the inspiration of Scripture, the Fall, and the great sacrifice of Christ for sin, it behoves us to see that we do not become accomplices with those who teach another gospel, and as it would seem from one writer, have avowedly another God."[6]

After facing and answering a few more objections raised to his previous articles, C. H. Spurgeon concluded: "What action is to be taken we leave to those who can see more plainly than we do what Israel ought to do. One thing is clear to us: we cannot be expected to meet in any Union which comprehends those whose teaching is on fundamental points exactly the reverse of that which we hold dear. Those who can do so will, no doubt, have weighty reasons with which to justify their action, and we will not sit in judgement upon those reasons; they may judge that a minority should not drive them out. To us it appears that there are many things upon which compromise is possible, but there are others in which it would be an act of treason to pretend to fellowship".[7]

This repudiation of any Union that was comprehensive enough to include the evangelical and the unorthodox led C. H. Spurgeon to consider his own relation to the Baptist Union meetings in Sheffield due for that very month. His decision not to go he clearly expressed: "With deep regret we abstain from assembling with those we dearly love and heartily respect, since it would involve us in a confederacy with those with whom we can have no communion in the Lord."[8]

At this point, however, C. H. Spurgeon did not resign from the Union. Rather, having stated his refusal to attend whilst the unorthodox were welcomed, he implied that he was ready to return if something was done. "Garibaldi complained that by the cession of Nice to France he had been made a foreigner in his native land; and our heart is burdened with a like sorrow; but those who banish us may yet be of another mind, and enable us to return."[9]

Nothing more of importance on the 'Downgrade' issue is to be found in the October issue of 'The Sword and Trowel'. The scene was set. C. H. Spurgeon would not attend the meetings of the Union until something was done about the unorthodox ministers. He had repeatedly conveyed his concern to the Union's officials publicly and privately. He now waited for some action.

The press, religious and secular, speculated on what C. H. Spurgeon wanted the Union to do and what his response to various actions would be.

The Baptist Union assembled at Sheffield and did nothing. The whole issue was ignored and the *status quo* was maintained. The 'Freeman' reported that at the meetings in Sheffield "the great joke was the Downgrade question. It did not seem to be treated very seriously."[10] This comment wounded C. H. Spurgeon deeply.

But not all found the controversy funny. As C. H. Spurgeon was about to prepare the November edition of 'The Sword and Trowel', a letter arrived which he incorporated in it with the following note:

"We have felt peculiar pleasure in a fraternal message from a band of London ministers who have not gone upon 'the Downgrade' and are not likely to do so. We thank them from our heart. The following resolution was passed with the most hearty unanimity by the representatives present at the half-yearly meeting of the Metropolitan Association of Strict Baptist Churches, held at Brentford, October 11th: 'Resolved that this meeting of Pastors and Delegates of the Metropolitan Association of Strict Baptist Churches, recognising and deploring the present widespread and awful departures from revealed truth, and believing the same to be largely traceable to the bold proclamation of error from some pulpits of various denominational bodies, desires to express its sympathy with Mr. C. H. Spurgeon, in the position he has taken in defence of the truth, and his uncompromising exposure of the evils referred to in his articles recently published entitled "The Downgrade" considering his action worthy of the highest commendation of all who are anxious to preserve and maintain the truths we hold in common."[11]

Such a letter heartened C. H. Spurgeon, especially

as so few were about to support him from his immediate Baptist constituency. In the later days of October he prepared the article for the November 'The Sword and Trowel' entitled "A fragment upon the Downgrade controversy".[12]

The sad opening paragraph reveals the weariness that C. H. Spurgeon felt in the fight for truth but the sense of duty that kept him going. He then sadly recounted the compromising attitude of the majority who would not acknowledge that the problem was great. He summarised their attitude exactly, "They are sorry that a few brethren go rather too far, but they are dear brethren still ... denominational peace must be kept up."[13]

C. H. Spurgeon affirmed his commitment to unity and liberty of conscience but "to pursue union at the expense of truth is treason to the Lord Jesus".[14] He warned against the danger of drifting into compromise and then being forced to justify it.

In four powerful paragraphs he then outlined the whole issue: "As a matter of fact, believers in Christ's atonement are now in declared religious union with those who make light of it; believers in Holy Scripture are in confederacy with those who deny plenary inspiration; those who hold evangelical doctrine are in open alliance with those who call the fall a fable, who deny the personality of the Holy Spirit, who call justification by faith immoral, and hold that there is another probation after death, and a future restitution for the lost. Yes, we have before us the wretched spectacle of professedly orthodox Christians publicly avowing their union with those who deny the faith, and scarcely

concealing their contempt for those who cannot be
guilty of such gross disloyalty to Christ. To be very
plain, we are unable to call those things Christian
Unions, they begin to look like Confederacies in
Evil."[15]

C. H. Spurgeon was aware that some might object
that there were things that could be done with the
unorthodox. He agreed. Men of differing theological
persuasions could work together for philanthropic
and political purposes. "But the case before us is that
of a distinctly religious communion, a professed
fellowship in Christ."[16]

He knew that he was being charged with heresy
hunting. He denied this. In this case "heresy is
avowed and is thrust forward in no diffident style".[17]
He was not looking for error. Error was on the
march!

To the assertion that he was an enemy of Christian
unity he replied: "The largest charity towards those
who are loyal to the Lord Jesus, and yet do not
see with us on secondary matters, is the duty of
all true Christians. But how are we to act towards
those who deny his vicarious sacrifice and ridicule
the great truth of justification by his righteousness?
These are not mistaken friends, but enemies of the
cross of Christ."[18]

Having answered these objections and set out his
position, C. H. Spurgeon summarised his conclusion
in one terse, italicized sentence: *"Fellowship with
known and vital error is participation in sin"*.[19]

He then expressed his desire that the unorthodox
would leave evangelical churches, unions and
fraternals; but as the Baptist Union would tolerate

them, whatever others might do, "We", he wrote, "retire at once and distinctly from the Baptist Union."[20] His resignation was announced.

To C. H. Spurgeon the Baptist Union was useless and powerless. "The Union, as at present constituted, has no disciplinary power, for it has no doctrinal basis whatever, and we see no reason why every form of belief and misbelief should not be comprehended in it so long as immersion only is acknowledged as baptism."[21]

To the suggestion that he should start a new denomination, he replied negatively. He argued that there were enough denominations, that organisations tended to be infiltrated and corrupt, and that self governing, self determining churches could fellowship without "hampering ropes" and "can keep their own coasts clear of invaders."[22]

The desire for independency on the part of C. H. Spurgeon was not a long term commitment to isolationism. The totality of his final paragraph needs to be noted: "In the isolation of independency, tempered by the love of the Spirit which binds us to all the faithful in Christ Jesus, we think the lovers of the Gospel will for the present find their immediate safety. Oh, that the day would come when, in a larger communion than any sect can offer, all those who are one in Christ may be able to blend in manifest unity! This can only come by the way of growing spiritual life, clearer light upon the one eternal truth, and a closer cleaving in all things to him who is the Head, even Christ Jesus."[23]

If present necessity required isolationism, future spiritual growth, commitment to the Word and to the

Lord would lead to non-sectarian unity among evangelicals.

With the article ready for the printer, C. H. Spurgeon wrote his letter of resignation to the Baptist Union. The same Dr. Booth, who had privately corresponded with C. H. Spurgeon and called on him to do something, now received a letter from him which caused him pain, alarm, confusion and wounding. It read:

"Dear Friend,

"I beg to intimate to you, as Secretary of the Baptist Union, that I must withdraw from that society. I do this with utmost regret, but I have no choice. The reasons are set forth in the Sword and Trowel for November, and I trust you will excuse my repeating them here. I beg you not to send anyone to me to ask for a reconsideration. I fear I have considered too long already. Certainly every hour of the day impresses upon me the conviction that I am moving none too soon. I wish to add that no personal pique or ill-will in the least degree has operated upon me. I have personally received more respect than I desire. It is on the highest grounds alone that I take this step, and you know that I have delayed it because I hoped for better things.

Yours always heartily,
C. H. Spurgeon."[24]

The notes in the November 'The Sword and Trowel' indicated that a tired C. H. Spurgeon had gone to the South of France to recuperate, tired and sick. He asked for no letters to be written to him and promised no answers to any received. He needed rest.

References
1. 'The Sword and Trowel' October 1887 pp. 509—515.
2. ibid. p. 509.
3. ibid. p. 511.
4. ibid. p. 513.
5. ibid. p. 513.
6. ibid. p. 513.
7. ibid. p. 515.
8. ibid. p. 515.
9. ibid. p. 515.
10. 'The Sword and Trowel' November 1887 p. 561.
11. ibid. p. 598.
12. ibid. pp. 557—560.
13. ibid. p. 557.
14. ibid. p. 558.
15. ibid. p. 558.
16. ibid. p. 559.
17. ibid. p. 559.
18. ibid. p. 559.
19. ibid. p. 559.
20. ibid. p. 560.
21. ibid. p. 560.
22. ibid. p. 560.
23. ibid. p. 560.
24. Cited in Bacon, E. W. (1982), *Spurgeon: 'Heir of the Puritans'.* Baker, p. 134.

7.
Censured

When the November issue of 'The Sword and Trowel'
was published, C. H. Spurgeon was resting in the
South of France. Not only did that issue include
his statement of resignation but an attack on the
'Freeman' newspaper for having reported the Baptist
Union Assembly in Sheffield as treating the 'Downgrade' controversy as a joke — "the big gooseberry
of the dull season".[1]

In an article by R. F. Weymouth, the 'Freeman'
and those whose activities it reported were asked
whether the apostles were joking when they said
that Christians were not to be conformed to this
world (Romans 12:1—2)? Was it amusing when
they said that those who departed from true doctrine
did not have God (II John:9)? Was Paul joking when
he told the Ephesian elders to warn their people
with tears (Acts 20:19)? Did our Lord laugh behind
his hand when he spoke of millstones being hung
around the necks of those who stumbled others and
they then being cast into the sea (Matthew 18:6)?[2]
The implications of the article were clear. If the delegates at the Baptist Union Assembly discussed the
'Downgrade' in their informal conversations as a
great joke, then they were mocking not Spurgeon,
who attacked worldliness and heresy, but our Lord
and his apostles.

This article elicited an apology from the 'Freeman'

47

for having published their article but it did not change the fact that to many accusations of worldliness and heresy were to be lightly dismissed and mocked. Ridicule has always been a powerful weapon by which to disarm the gullible. Once men laughed at funny Mr. Hitler; they do so no more!

Soon after his resignation from the Baptist Union, C. H. Spurgeon had the joy of receiving a resolution from his church, the Metropolitan Tabernacle, which affirmed their sympathy and support of him in his actions. In various resolutions they assured him that what he had done was necessary and correct and expressed their hope that ultimately it would aid the cause of true Christian unity.

Additional support came from a number of ministers, including Robert Shindler, who also resigned from the Union. But these encouragements were far outnumbered by those who would not follow his example, who withdrew financial support from the institutions in which he was involved, who wrote letters to him criticizing him, or who misinterpreted him in print. Resignation was no light thing for C. H. Spurgeon, but he consoled himself in that his "heartiest sympathizers" were in his own church.[3]

Among those who wrote to C. H. Spurgeon about his resignation was Dr. Culross, the 1887 President of the Baptist Union. The letter was kind and polite, and C. H. Spurgeon replied in a similar respectful vein. The points made in his letter are of considerable importance.[4] They were:

1. His only dispute with the evangelicals in the Union was their decision to stay in the Union. This

would not stop C. H. Spurgeon co-operating with
them as individuals in a fight against modernism.

2. He did not see any way of returning to the
Union and requested no special treatment. The
Union was doomed because it had no formal creed
and, therefore, no way of excluding the unorthodox.

3. He saw the future strength of the unorthodox
as inevitably increasing, and the compromised evangelicals being saddened by this but powerless to
stop it.

4. He had repeatedly publicly and privately asked
the officials of the Union to deal with the problem
and had only acted after they failed to do so.

5. He would continue personal fellowship with
the evangelicals but could not accept their fellowship with the unorthodox. He felt no fellowship
with the unorthodox at all.

6. The Baptist Union was so committed to a
loose policy that it was useless dealing with it.

This letter gives further insight into C. H.
Spurgeon's reasons for resignation. He knew that
the unorthodox had so infiltrated the Union that
the attainment of a credal standard that would
actually exclude them was an impossibility. As
the unorthodox, therefore, were bound to stay in
the Union for the foreseeable future, if he stayed
he would have to fellowship with them. This he
would not do.

As for those evangelicals who stayed in the Union,
he considered them short-sighted, unperceptive,
doomed to failure and disappointment and compromised. He did not question their motives but
their wisdom. He did not desire to cut them off as

he cut off fellowship from the unorthodox. He would have fellowship with them, but not in a comprehensive union.

In preparing the December issue of 'The Sword and Trowel', C. H. Spurgeon included four things that had reference to the 'Downgrade' controversy: his editorial, an article on worldliness by J. H. Norton, the supportive letters of his own church, and his comments on the controversy.

In the first of these, the editorial entitled "Restoration of Truth and Revival",[5] C. H. Spurgeon affirmed his belief that unless there was a revival by which truth would be made to prevail over error "the churches will descend until error and ungodliness swallow them up."[6]

Alongside this he recognised human responsibility: "We cannot expect a gracious revival till we are clear of complicity with the deadening influences which are all around us".[7] These deadening influences he saw as worldliness and false doctrine — the obsession with amusements rather than prayer, novelty rather than solidity. Hence this inclusion of the article by J. Norton on worldly amusements.

C. H. Spurgeon observed that more and more churches were interested in plays, theatre, and amusement than in prayer and the promotion of godliness. He did not see this trend as coincidental. "It is clear to everyone who is willing to see it that laxity of doctrine is either the parent of worldliness, or is in some other way very near akin to it. The men who give up the old faith are the same persons who plead for latitude as to general conduct."[8] He noticed that "liberal divines . . . gain a certain popularity by pandering to prevailing tastes."[9]

He called for the restatement of fundamental
truths, and special prayer for God's blessing. He
rejected the call to form a new church grouping for
a call to prayer. "Pray without ceasing, and preach
the faithful Word in clearer terms than ever."[10]

In his notes for December, C. H. Spurgeon had to
deal with two responses:

1. that he was simply restating the Calvinism/
Arminianism debate, and
2. that to withdraw from error was contrary to
the love required by our Lord.

To the first accusation he replied by a brusque
denial: "Certain antagonists have tried to represent
the Downgrade controversy as a revival of the old
feud between Calvinists and Arminians. It is nothing
of the kind. Many evangelical Arminians are as
earnestly on our side as men can be. We do not
conceal our Calvinism in the least; but this conflict
is for truths that are common to all believers. This
is no battle over words, but it deals with the eternal
verities — those foundation truths which belong not
exclusively to this party or that. It is of no use
attempting to drag this red herring across our
path."[11]

He then distinguished between disputes within
evangelicalism such as the Calvinist/Arminian debate
and disputes with its enemies such as the modernists.
"We can argue other points and maintain Christian
harmony at the same time; but with those who treat
the Bible as waste paper, and regard the death of
Christ as no substitution, we have no desire for
fellowship".[12]

C. H. Spurgeon's reply to those who accused him
of being uncharitable was strongly worded: "The
barefaced manner in which certain persons assert
that to separate from men who hold vital errors is
contrary to the mind of Christ would be amusing
if it were not saddening. They write as if such a
Book as the New Testament were not in existence:
they evidently decide what the mind of Christ ought
to be without referring to such poor creatures as the
Apostles. As for us we think more of Paul and John
than of the whole Body of modern thinkers. What
saith the Scriptures?"[13] He then quoted II John
10–11 and Galatians 1:8–9 and continued: "The
spirit of Scripture is one, and therefore we may be
sure that decision for truth and separation from the
erring are in full consistency with the charity of
1 Corinthians 13, to which we are so continually
pointed. It is true charity to those who err to refuse
to aid and abet them in their errors. 'Charity' sounds
very prettily in the mouths of those who wish to
screen themselves, but, if they had exercised it in
the past, they might not have driven us out from
among the people to whom we naturally belong."[14]

In his concluding comments, C. H. Spurgeon
pessimistically (although accurately) prophesied that
few would follow him out of the Union. He expressed
the hope that those who stayed in would "Resolve
that reform shall be carried out and truth vindi-
cated".[15] In this he was to be sorely disappointed.

After the December issue of 'The Sword and
Trowel' had been published, eighty of the hundred
members of the Baptist Union Council met on 13th
December to discuss the crisis created by C. H.
Spurgeon's resignation.

Two evangelicals presented motions for acceptance. Dr. Angus proposed that the Union adopt a declaration of evangelical faith and that this should be accompanied by a confident assertion of the Union's theological soundness. Effectively, it was a request to declare the Union evangelical in belief and fact. If it had been accepted it would have been an outright denial of the problem that existed! Acceptance or rejection was deferred.

The second motion proposed by James Spurgeon, Charles' brother, proposed the adoption of the doctrinal basis of the Evangelical Alliance. If this had been adopted it would have declared the Union as unequivocally evangelical but it would not have necessarily excluded anyone unless they chose to exclude themselves. Discussion was again deferred.

The officers of the Union, and especially Dr. Booth, denied having received any formal charges from C. H. Spurgeon which should have been brought to the Council but suggested that a scriptural procedure (!) would be to interview C. H. Spurgeon in line with our Lord's teaching in Matthew 18:15 and to travel to Mentone in the South of France if necessary to do this.

When C. H. Spurgeon was informed of the Council meeting and what had occurred he was saddened and angry. He wrote to 'The Baptist' and to his congregation rejecting the suggestion that he had acted dishonestly in not making formal and specific charges to the Council. He had made many such charges. His brother James had reported the Council meeting as "horrible" and "an affray" which he had left in indignation when C. H. Spurgeon's truthfulness was questioned.[16]

When C. H. Spurgeon was informed by telegram from Dr. Booth that in accordance with Matthew 18:15 a deputation of four theological doctors was coming to see him, he put them off until his return to England in January. He was very suspicious about the purpose of the meeting. He felt that far from being an attempt to bring about peace and harmony, they in fact were trying to present him as awkward or as he put it "to fix on me the odium of being implacable".[17]

He recognised also the deceitfulness of Dr. Booth and others in coming to see him according to Matthew 18:15 to hear his grievance as if they had never heard it before. To his wife he wrote, "For Dr. Booth to say I never complained is amazing"[18] and "What a farce about my seeing these brethren, privately, accordingly to Matthew 18:15. Why, I saw the Secretary and President again and again; and then I printed my plaint and only left the Union when nothing could be done."[19]

C. H. Spurgeon had the proof he needed to reveal the double-dealing of Dr. Booth. He had the letters Dr. Booth had written to him which included the names of those Dr. Booth accused of unorthodoxy and the unorthodox sections of their sermons he had sent to C. H. Spurgeon with a request for action. He also had copies of his own letters in reply.

C. H. Spurgeon wrote to Dr. Booth stating his intention to hand over these letters. Dr. Booth replied that such action was improper as the correspondence was private. C. H. Spurgeon — ever the Christian gentleman — agreed not to make the letters public. It was chivalrous but his biggest mistake.

Without the publication of the letters the accusation that he had never made formal protests to the Union could be upheld. Courtesy and respect for confidentiality undermined his credibility in the discussions that followed. That Dr. Booth should have tied C. H. Spurgeon's hands by appealing to confidentiality means "that the responsibility for the subsequent unfortunate proceedings rests squarely with Booth".[20]

The January edition of 'The Sword and Trowel' was prepared before C. H. Spurgeon received news of the Baptist Union Council's decision,[21] and contains little direct reference to the 'Downgrade' issue although two of the articles by J. Kemp and E. Holt were attacks on the new gospel and the new worldliness at the heart of the 'Downgrade'. In his notes C. H. Spurgeon mentioned the cheering effect of support and the saddening effect of defection.[22]

In his notes, however, he made a vitally important comment. He knew that some faithful evangelical men would stay in the Union in order to gain it for evangelicalism. Whilst disagreeing with this action, he refused to break fellowship with those who stayed in the Union for the period of the battle that was to be waged until the Annual Assembly. "To our faithful brethren we would say that, whatever they may choose to do as to the Baptist Union will not imperil our hearty union with each other. One by leaving and another by remaining may be aiming at the same end."[23]

C. H. Spurgeon had left the Union because he did not believe the unorthodox would be dislodged. He recognised, however, that other brethren who were

equally opposed to the unorthodox were not so
pessimistic. They did believe that something could
be done. C. H. Spurgeon reasoned that they were
working for the same end as he was.

However, in what followed he made it clear that
to him there was only a limited period in which it
was possible for the faithful to remain in the Union.
"One by leaving and another by remaining may both
be aiming at the same end. This is true while we are
writing; but if it be once definitely decided that
Universalists, rejectors of the Atonement, and persons
who do not regard the Holy Scripture as the infallible
authority in doctrine, are to remain in the Union,
then it will not be an open question. The duty of
Christian men will surely then be clear enough."[24]

The principle enunciated by C. H. Spurgeon here
is of profound importance. He recognised that the
Baptist Union had begun as an evangelical group
and had decided at that time that as it was evangelical it needed no credal basis. As time had passed
it had been infiltrated by the unorthodox. It was in
the throes of deciding what to do with the unorthodox. C. H. Spurgeon felt it could do nothing about
them and so had withdrawn from them. Others felt
that the cause was not lost. The establishing of the
Union as an evangelical body excluding the unorthodox could be attained. C. H. Spurgeon promised
fellowship to those aiming to do this. However, if
they lost, if they were not able to exclude the unorthodox, then their duty was clear. They also
would have to leave the Union.

It must be clear from this that C. H. Spurgeon
was not advocating an 'in it to win it' philosophy.

He was only willing to support evangelicals remaining in denominations and unions while the issue of the acceptance of the unorthodox was being debated. Once it was seen that the unorthodox were acceptable, secession was a clear duty.

On his return from the South of France to England in the early days of January, C. H. Spurgeon received a welcome full of "great heartiness and enthusiasm" from his church at the Metropolitan Tabernacle.

On the 13th January, Drs. Culross, Clifford and Booth met with C. H. Spurgeon at the Tabernacle to "follow through Matthew 18:15" and entered into difficult discussions. C. H. Spurgeon made a last attempt to get the Council to adopt a clear evangelical basis of faith similar to that of the Evangelical Alliance so that the unorthodox would have to depart. But all ideas of a credal statement were rejected.

When he was pressed to name the unorthodox ministers and present his evidence he refused because Dr. Booth would not permit his letters to be divulged and without a credal basis for the Union no-one could be excluded anyway!

Within a few days[26] the Baptist Union Council met and passed a resolution accepting C. H. Spurgeon's resignation. But it did not stop there. It also passed a second resolution which read: "That the Council recognises the gravity of the charges which Mr. Spurgeon has brought against the Union previous to and since his withdrawal. It considers that the public and general manner in which they have been made reflects on the whole body and exposes to suspicion brethren who love the truth

as dearly as he does. And, as Mr. Spurgeon declined
to give the names of those to whom he intended
them to apply, and the evidence supporting them,
those charges in the judgement of the Council ought
not to have been made."[27]

Men like J. G. Greenhough, who were unorthodox,
spoke in favour of this motion, but so did some of
C. H. Spurgeon's friends. Only five Council members
opposed it including James Spurgeon. This resolution
was interpreted as a censure of C. H. Spurgeon.

In preparing the February edition of 'The Sword
and Trowel', C. H. Spurgeon included an article
entitled "The Baptist Union Censure".[28] He began
by appealing to the faithful to judge between him
and the Council of the Baptist Union.

He explained why he had not made any specific
charges against members of the Baptist Union. This
was due to the fact that the Union's constitution
required nothing more than the acceptance of immersion as Christian baptism for membership. Unless a
person deviated on baptism he could not be excluded.
Any proven charges of heresy on other points could
not be acted upon and so it was useless to specify
the charges.

He suggested that this censure was the real purpose
of the visit of the delegation of the Baptist Union
Council. That had been an ostensibly biblical action
to pave the way for censure. He accused the delegation of having this secret intention all the time.

He then made clear what he had encouraged the
delegation to do: "I would like all Christendom
to know that all I asked of the Union was that it
be formed on a Scriptural basis, and that I never

sought to intrude upon it any Calvinistic or other
personal creed, but only that form of belief which
has been accepted for many years by the Evangelical
Alliance which includes members of well nigh all
Christian communities."[29]

He then reported the response he had received:
"To this it was replied that there is an objection
to any creed whatever."[30] C. H. Spurgeon then
reasoned as to why this answer was foolish. He
pointed out that Baptists had a tradition of creeds;
that the Baptist Union had a creed on baptism (if
nothing else!); that the churches and colleges in the
Baptist Union had creeds; and that a creed in plain
language expressing the truth of scripture is an aid
to men in their relationship with God, not a hindrance. All men in fact have a creed whether they
write it out or not. Even "unbelief is, in a sense,
a creed".[31]

Following this statement C. H. Spurgeon stated
why he believed there was such an objection to
creeds in the Baptist Union Council. "The objection
to a creed is a very pleasant way of concealing objection to discipline, and a desire for latitudinarianism.
What is wished for is a Union which will, like Noah's
ark, afford shelter both for the clean and for the
unclean."[32]

To the objection that the Baptist Union's statement on baptism was a sufficient basis for a union,
C. H. Spurgeon replied: "Surely to be a Baptist is
not everything. If I disagree with a man on ninety-
nine points but happen to be one with him in baptism, this can never furnish such ground of unity
as I have with another with whom I believe in ninety-

nine points and only happen to differ upon one
ordinance."[33]

He concluded that it might be best to take the
Baptist Union apart and start again. He sympathised
with those who thought they could make the Union
"an avowedly Evangelical body on the old lines of
faith",[34] but he had no confidence in their success.
Now he was outside the Union he was no longer
hampered by it but would continue to expose doctrinal declension wherever it appeared.

In his notes C. H. Spurgeon pointed out that in
getting rid of him, "The offensive personage",[35]
the Union had not got rid of its own uncertain
position on various false doctrines. As there were
church members and council members who believed
that sinners had a second chance of salvation after
death, was this, or was this not, a belief of the Union?
Here C. H. Spurgeon attacked, without naming
him, the prominent Baptist Dr. Samuel Cox who
"had made himself one of the best known and
ablest exponents of universal restoration".[36]

C. H. Spurgeon made it clear that he was not
asking for heresy trials but that the Union should
"tell the world what it believes . . . It could clear
its somewhat blurred reputation if it passed a resolution setting forth that it rejected the dream of future
probation and restoration as unscriptural, unprotest-
ant and a stranger among Baptists."[37]

Elsewhere in the February issue, through an article
by Robert Shindler, C. H. Spurgeon made clear that
his rejection of those doctrines was in accord with
that of the evangelical faith throughout the ages.[38]
He also insisted that confrontation with error was

the only course open to the evangelical. Compromise must be rejected.

In calling on the Baptist Union Council to join him in a clear repudiation of this error, C. H. Spurgeon made clear what his purpose was. "If there be certain definite doctrines laid down, men who honestly differ will go; and if they do not their remaining will not be the fault of their brethren."[39] He saw a clear-cut creed as forcing resignation on the dissenters.

However, he also recognised that the Baptist Union Council as constituted was not to be trusted to give a clear-cut creed. If it accepted any creed at all it would be the sort of creed that could have a number of interpretations. "It might say one thing, and mean another."[40] C. H. Spurgeon was far-sighted enough to guess what the Council would do. They would adopt a creed, but one so vague that everyone would be happy with it. His expectation was entirely correct, as we shall see.

Censured and abused, he concluded: "We look for a gracious revival as the true antidote for the new unbelief. The truth is being preached more boldly already and we may look for corresponding fruit. Prayer goes up to God day and night and a blessing must come as a result of it."[41]

References
1. 'The Sword and Trowel' November 1887 p. 561.
2. ibid. pp. 562–563.
3. 'The Sword and Trowel' December 1887 p. 641.
4. Spurgeon's Autobiography: *The Full Harvest* (1973) Banner of Truth, pp. 478–479.

5.   'The Sword and Trowel' December 1887 pp. 605–607.
6.   ibid. p. 605.
7.   ibid. p. 605.
8.   ibid. p. 606.
9.   ibid. p. 606.
10.   ibid. p. 607.
11.   ibid. p. 642.
12.   ibid. p. 642.
13.   ibid. p. 642.
14.   ibid. p. 642.
15.   ibid. p. 642.
16.   *The Full Harvest* p. 472.
17.   'The Sword and Trowel' December 1887 p. 472.
18.   ibid. p. 472.
19.   ibid. p. 471.
20.   Bacon, E. W. op. cit. p. 136.
21.   'The Sword and Trowel' January 1888 p. 44.
22.   ibid. p. 44.
23.   ibid. p. 44.
24.   ibid. p. 44.
25.   'The Sword and Trowel' February 1888 p. 92.
26.   According to I. Murray, January 18th, according to E. W. Bacon,
      January 15th.
27.   Reported Bacon, E. W. op. cit. p. 137.
28.   'The Sword and Trowel' February 1888 pp. 81–83.
29.   ibid. p. 82.
30.   ibid. p. 82.
31.   ibid. p. 82.
32.   ibid. p. 82.
33.   ibid. p. 83.
34.   ibid. p. 83.
35.   ibid. p. 91.
36.   Underwood op. cit. p. 230.
37.   'The Sword and Trowel' February 1888 p.
38.   ibid. pp. 62–66.
39.   ibid. p. 91.
40.   ibid. p. 91.
41.   ibid. p. 91.

8.
A creed for all and none

C. H. Spurgeon prepared the March issue of 'The Sword and Trowel' before the February meeting of the Council of the Baptist Union.[1] In it he included an article by Robert Shindler in which it was demonstrated that evangelical Baptists had in past centuries had to fight unorthodoxy, and that where they could not prevail against it they had considered it their duty to separate from it. Mr. Shindler implied thereby that the Baptists of his day could not use either scripture or Baptist church history to attack the action of C. H. Spurgeon and his colleagues because separation from error was not schism but a necessary duty.[2]

In his notes for the March issue, C. H. Spurgeon rejoiced in the letters of support received from various Australasian Baptists, from many of the men connected with the College of which he was the President and especially from his own church meeting. Sadly he noted the defection of some College men from the truth but was encouraged because the controversy had spurred others on to greater earnestness in prayer and preaching.[3]

Most important of all, however, were his comments directed towards the February meeting of the Council of the Baptist Union. He knew that there was talk of the acceptance of a credal basis for the Union. However, he had grave doubts about the

creed that might be adopted. His doubts arose from
the fact that the creed would be the product of a
Council of men rather than something carefully
constructed. His feelings about committee creeds
and decisions were summarised in a forceful manner:
"A committee is a many-headed, many-tongued
thing, and its action is apt to be the result of internal
compromise or of momentary impetuosity rather
than of quiet sober thought. In fact, there is no
accounting for what may come out of the lucubra-
tions of a hundred men."[4]

This fear that the creed would be the product
of compromise caused C. H. Spurgeon to conclude:
"So far as we can judge, there is no likelihood whatever that the Baptist Union will obtain a Scriptural
Basis."[5]

He had warned in previous articles of the way that
men made the meaning of words elastic so that no
real meaning could be attached to them. He returned
to this theme: "I must, however, protest against anyone saying that he believes orthodox doctrine 'but
not in Mr. Spurgeon's sense'. I believe these doctrines, as far as I know, in the common and usual
sense attached to them by the general usage of
Christendom. Theological terms ought to be understood and used only in their general and usual meaning."[6]

He then applied this principle to the specific issue
of the creed that the Council might adopt: "Whatever the Council does, let it above all things avoid
the use of language which could legitimately have
two meanings contrary to each other. Let us be plain
and outspoken. There are grave differences — let

them be avowed honestly. Why should any man be ashamed to do so? Policy must not be our guide, nor the wish to retain this party or that. Right is safe, and compromise by the use of double meanings can never in the long run be wise."[7]

C. H. Spurgeon had with an almost uncanny insight predicted the precise way in which the Council and ultimately the Assembly would resolve its differences. At the Council meeting of the Baptist Union on 21st February, Dr. Angus presented a declaration of faith for consideration.

The unorthodox led by S. G. Green and J. G. Greenhough subjected Dr. Angus' declaration to much criticism. Dr. Clifford came to the rescue with a preamble that made the declaration meaningless. Whereas the declaration set out six doctrines in a skeletal form, the preamble stated: "First, that the doctrinal beliefs of the Union are and must be determined by the doctrinal beliefs of the Churches and Associations of which the Union is composed. Secondly, that the Council of the Union therefore disclaims altogether any authority to formulate a new and additional standard of theological belief as a band of union to which assent shall be required."[8]

This preamble simply stated that the doctrines were believed in the sense understood in the churches and that no additional creed was required. C. H. Spurgeon's whole point was that in those churches and associations there were a variety of beliefs and interpretations. The preamble stated that the Union held to the truths in line with the beliefs of the evangelicals and the unorthodox! In other words, it asserted the confusion and mixture of the *status quo*. As E. W. Bacon correctly stated, "The only firm basis for faith, and the standard of testing it, was the Holy Scriptures to which Spurgeon appealed. The Baptist Union gave its whole case away by setting up the notions of men as the standard instead of the inspired Word of God."[9]

When the Council accepted the declaration and the preamble, James Spurgeon — C. H. Spurgeon's brother — was among its supporters. C. H. Spurgeon, however, believed his brother to have made a great mistake.

In March, C. H. Spurgeon prepared the April issue of 'The Sword and Trowel'. He knew that on the 23rd April the Baptist Union Assembly would meet and would decide on the issue of the creed. In the light of this his editorial was entitled "Progressive Theology".[10]

In this editorial C. H. Spurgeon noted with a measure of satisfaction that the 'Downgrade' controversy had emboldened many men to speak out in favour of unorthodoxy and thus to reveal their true beliefs. His satisfaction arose from the fact that "it is better for us to know where we are and with whom we are associating".[11]

He then considered the 'discoveries' of modern unorthodoxy and found them to be old heresies dressed up in new clothes. He turned to the attitude of those who wanted to maintain the *status quo* in the Union and allow evangelicals and the unorthodox to remain in fellowship: "Pan-indifferentism is rising like the tide; who can hinder it? We are all to be one, even though we agree in next to nothing. It is a

breach of brotherly love to denounce error. Hail,
holy charity! Black is white; and white is black. The
false is true; the true is false; the true and false are
one . . . In order to maintain an open union let us
fight as far as dear life against any form of sound
words, since it might restrain our liberty to deny the
doctrines of the Word of God."[12]

C. H. Spurgeon then expressed the hope that his
stand against error might encourage some waverers,
and expressed his confidence that in the end the
truth would prevail in spite of the policies of men.

He again encouraged the Baptist Union Assembly
to accept an "Evangelical basis . . . but if this is not
done, other and stronger measures must be taken,
which will enable faithful men to bear their testimony without having it marred by their fellowship
with evil."[13] Either the purifying process had to
begin or else evangelicals should "come forth from
the baseless Union and separate themselves for the
defence of the truth of God".[14]

Later in the same issue C. H. Spurgeon included
a strident poem by A. Midlane entitled "Treason in
the Camp".[15] In his notes he again asserted his
belief that the Union had to adopt an evangelical
basis. "We have come to the parting of the ways and
the old school and the new cannot go much further
in company; nor ought they to do so. Let them
part with as little friction as possible."[16]

Before the Assembly C. H. Spurgeon had the
Pastor's College Conference to address and, therefore, he prepared the May issue of 'The Sword and
Trowel' in the first half of April. It is evident that
he was aware by this time of the proposed creed

and its preamble. He again asserted that his only interest was to gain a clear statement on the central truths of revelation from the Union. "We only asked that the grosser forms of error should not be tolerated within the bounds of the Christian body to which we belonged. We thought the request a reasonable one, and to obtain it we proposed a form of sound words to be the basis of union."[17]

With reference to the proposed creed he commented, "Even now that body does not like distinctly to refuse, or honestly to yield, the demand; and so it balances sentences, discusses everything except the main question, and proffers a base imitation of a declaration in lieu of that which is sought from it. Writing before the Annual Meeting, we write hopelessly."[18]

These comments, of course, were not going to be read until after the Assembly! They express clearly C. H. Spurgeon's view of the likely outcome. A creed would be accepted but it would be a meaningless emasculated mass of double meanings and would establish the *status quo*.

In the same issue in his editorial "Remarks on Inspiration",[19] C. H. Spurgeon stated that the doctrine of inspiration was the turning point of the battle. He would fellowship with a brother who sincerely misinterpreted the word of God and needed help to understand it properly "but we must part company altogether with the errorist, who overrides prophets and apostles, and practically regards his own inspiration as superior to theirs".[20]

He saw the unorthodox as aiming to "take our Bibles from us"[21] and then proceeded to give a spirited defence of the doctrine of inspiration and to reaffirm it. Later in the same issue there was a short paragraph on "Why creeds are necessary" by Principal Harper[22] which required men not only to use biblical language but to use it in a biblical sense.

On 17th April C. H. Spurgeon addressed the "Pastor's College Evangelical Association". This address was later printed in the June and July issues of 'The Sword and Trowel' under the title "The Evils of the Present Time"[23], and with a footnote which read, "Although this was delivered before the resolution of the Baptist Union nothing has occurred to require any softening, but much to emphasise it. The evils spoken of were at first denied, but surely none can now question that they exist, abound and triumph."[24]

In opening his address, C. H. Spurgeon stated his intention to say little directly about the forthcoming Assembly, and assured his hearers he was not interested in personalities but only with contending for the faith and fighting deadly error. He then listed the errors of the day as:

1. The great evil of questioning fundamental truth.
2. The great evil of misrepresenting and distorting evangelical beliefs.
3. The great evil of failing to stand for the truth and to denounce error and sin.
4. The great evil of the insatiable desire for amusements.
5. The great evil of lack of intense piety in many of the churches.
6. The great evil of hardheartedness amongst gospel hearers.

In fact in this address he was outlining the very malaise at the heart of the whole 'Downgrade' controversy. He then called on the preachers to:

1. Have as their chief end the glorifying of God.
2. Have an intense desire to build up the church.
3. Be better men.
4. Get clearer views of what they believe.
5. Have more faith.
6. Have more love for souls.
7. Have a more thorough spirit of self-sacrifice.
8. Go over the fundamental truths with their hearers very carefully.
9. Labour distinctly for the immediate salvation of their hearers.
10. Inculcate with all their might the practice of holiness.
11. Be careful about the admission of members into the church.
12. Separate entirely from those likely to cause spiritual injury.
13. Bind themselves together more closely.
14. Remember that past bad times have been followed by good times.
15. Make the most of prayer.

In this lengthy address C. H. Spurgeon again applied the separatist principles he had formed in the twelfth and thirteenth points. Under the twelfth he said: "As to yourselves, I would recommend entire separation from those who would be likely to injure your spiritual life. I would no more associate with a man who denied the faith than with a drunkard or a thief. I would guard my spirituals as jealously as my morals. A loyal man is not at home in the company of traitors. There are associations with the ungodly into which we must needs go, unless we get out of the world altogether; but there are others which are optional, and here we should dare to be scrupulous. A godly minister once said of a certain preacher 'I would not permit such a man to enter my pulpit. I am as jealous of my pulpit as of my bed'. I do not think he was too rigid. We should guard ourselves against compromising the truth of God by association with those who do not hold it, especially at such a time as this."[25]

But under the thirteenth point he stressed the positive side of separation from error. "We must bind ourselves more closely together, and seek to render help to each other, and to all who are of the same mind in the Lord. Denominational divisions sink in the presence of the truth of God. To my mind, the grand distinction to be now observed is found in evangelical doctrine, of which our Lord's substitutionary sacrifice is the centre and the soul. Where there are faithful brethren struggling we ought to lay ourselves out to help them for they are sure to be the objects of inveterate opposition. Lovers of the old faith should stand shoulder to shoulder, to remove the injustice of the past, and frustrate the opposition of the future. The struggle before us is severe; let us, at any rate, economize our strength by union."[26]

The fateful day of Assembly arrived on 23rd April 1888 at the City Temple. The church was full. The motion before the Assembly read: "Whilst expressly disavowing and disallowing any power to control belief or to restrict enquiry, yet in view of the uneasiness produced in the churches by recent discussions, and to show our agreement with one another and with our fellow Christians on the great truths of the Gospel, the Council deem it right to say that:

A. Baptised in the name of the Father, and of the Son and of the Holy Ghost, we have avowed repentance towards God and faith in the Lord Jesus Christ – the very elements of a new life; as in the Supper we avow our Union with one another, while partaking of the symbol of the Body of our Lord, broken for us, and of the Blood shed for the remission of sins. The Union, therefore, is an association of Churches and ministers, professing not only to believe the facts and doctrines of the Gospel, but to have undergone the spiritual change expressed or implied in them. This change is the fundamental principle of our Church life.

B. The following facts and doctrines are commonly believed by the Churches of the Union:

1. The Divine Inspiration and Authority of the Holy Scripture as the supreme and sufficient rule of our faith and practice; and the right and duty of individual judgement in the interpretation of it.

2. The fallen and sinful nature of man.

3. The Deity, the Incarnation, the Resurrection of the Lord Jesus Christ, and His Sacrificial and Mediatorial work.

4. Justification by faith – a faith that works by love and produces holiness.

5. The work of the Holy Spirit in the conversion of sinners and in the sanctification of all who believe.

6. The Resurrection, the Judgement at the Last Day, according to the Words of our Lord in Matthew 25:46.

Footnote: it should be stated, as a historical fact, that there have been brethren in the Union, working cordially with it, who, while reverently bowing to the authority of Holy Scripture, and rejecting the doctrine of Purgatory and Universalism, have not held the common interpretation of these words of our Lord."[27]

A careful study of this statement reveals its glowing weaknesses. The preamble rejects the idea of a doctrinal test. It leaves the door open for free enquiry. The footnote accepts the fact of variation in belief in the eternal state. It had to, as some of the leading Baptists were great exponents of the "larger hope" which transformed the doctrine of hell into nothing.

E. W. Bacon has also noted that the statements of the declaration "are stated in most general terms and several are capable of widely different interpretations. Further, nothing whatever is said of the Substitutionary Atonement of Christ, the Virgin Birth, the Holy Trinity . . . or the Second Advent of Christ. The phrase justification by faith has the vital word 'only' omitted."[28]

The fact that this declaration was meaningless as a barrier to the unorthodox was further evidenced by the fact that its acceptance was proposed by Rev. Charles Williams of Accrington. In a bitter speech hostile to C. H. Spurgeon "he quoted Tennyson in favour of a liberal theology and justification of Doubt".[29] He had to, of course, for he rejected the inerrancy of Scripture.[30]

Incredibly, James Spurgeon seconded the motion, although in so doing he made it clear he was only giving support to the motion, not to the proposer's speech.

When Dr. Clifford, who himself rejected inerrancy,[31] put the motion to the meeting, it was accepted by 2000 votes in favour to 7 against. Cheering and scenes of joy greeted the vote. Paper unity had been accomplished amongst the Baptists.

James Spurgeon rushed to tell his brother the good news of the "victory". An "evangelical" credal statement had been accepted by the Baptist Union. C. H. Spurgeon was not convinced.

Knowing that the May issue of 'The Sword and Trowel' would soon be available with its comments about his expectation that the Baptist Union would do nothing and that the case was hopeless, C. H. Spurgeon published an insert to give his comments on the Assembly decision to accompany that edition.

In those comments, written on 27th April, C. H. Spurgeon recognised that the Council had tried to draw up a conciliatory document and regretted any bitterness in his comments about the hopelessness of expecting good from them. He recognised that his brother felt he had gained a great victory but said, "I have very serious doubts as to the practical value of what is gained, but I am sure that my brother did what he believed to be best for the cause of truth . . . Wherein I feel compelled to differ it will be with sincere regret . . . In differing from him I do only that which involves no disagreement of heart: we are equally earnest for the selfsame thing."[32]

C. H. Spurgeon then explained that he had to

reject the declaration because the speech of its proposer and the content of the footnote to the sixth
doctrine showed its true nature. The terms were
being given a double meaning even before they had
been accepted. He, therefore, reaffirmed that he was
finished with the Union and would continue to shun
union with the unorthodox. He concluded: "I could
have wished that instead of saving the Union, or
even purifying it, the more prominent thought had
been to conform everything to the Word of the
Lord."[33]

C. H. Spurgeon's disappointment in his brother
is reflected in a letter he wrote to a friend on 26th
April. "My brother thinks he has gained a great
victory, but I believe we are hopelessly sold. I feel
heart-broken. Certainly he has done the very opposite
of what I should have done. Yet he is not to be
blamed, for he followed his best judgement. Pray
for me that my faith fail not."[34]

In preparing the June 'The Sword and Trowel'
during May, C. H. Spurgeon published his April
address to the College to which he had already
referred, a short article against the idea of progressive theology, and his notes.

In his notes he commended the Baptist Union
for wanting to do something to clear itself of the
charges made against it, but soon showed the shallow-
ness of its intentions by its actions. "But what has
it done? The resolution, with its footnote, with the
interpretation of its mover, and the re-election of
the old council, fairly represent the utmost that
would be done when everybody was in his best
humour. Is it satisfactory? Does anybody understand

it in the same sense as anybody else? Does not
the whole virtue of the thing lie in its pleasing both
sides a little? And is not this the vice and the condemnation of it?"[35]

To the query of those who asked whether or not
C. H. Spurgeon now had a way to return and fight
the battle on the basis of the declaration, he replied:
"My course has been made clear by what has been
done. I was afraid from the beginning that the
reform of the Baptist Union was hopeless and therefore I resigned. I am far more sure of it now, and
should never dream under any circumstance of
returning. Those who think it right to remain in
such a fellowship will do so, but there are a few
others who will judge differently, and will act upon
their convictions. At any rate, whether any others
do so or not, I have felt the power of the text 'Come
out from among them and be ye separate' and have
quitted both Union and Association once for all."[36]

As to the suggestion that a new union of separated
churches should be formed, C. H. Spurgeon replied:
"The instinct of the gracious life is to seek congenial
communion, and hence the necessity of some form
of fellowship for ourselves and our churches will
suggest itself to those who sorrowfully come forth
from the old camp. To institute such a thing formally and ask persons to join it would be folly; it
must grow up of itself — by the demand of those
who desire it, and then it will be true and lasting.
I do not, therefore, move in this direction till I hear
from other brethren of like mind that they desire
to do so. It will not harm us to abide alone for a
little while till we see where we are; and then,

whether we are few or many, we can unite to help our poorer brethren and to conserve the faith. Our desire is not to oppose others but that we may strengthen each other's hand in the Lord. Utterly isolated church life would have its evils, and in true union there will not only be strength but joy. This will come in due time if it be the Lord's will."[37]

From this time onwards until his death in 1892, C. H. Spurgeon continued to preach and to write about the 'Downgrade', but he did so as a man with few real supporters. He did not add much to the principles he had set out throughout the controversy in his later writings. He simply amassed more and more evidence of defection from the truth of scripture and became increasingly isolated because few would stand with him, and soon he died; in part this was because of the immense pressures of standing against the prevailing tide of unorthodoxy.

In an article entitled "Attempts at the Impossible" in the December edition of 'The Sword and Trowel',[38] C. H. Spurgeon said, "There are now two parties in the religious world, and a great mixed multitude who from various causes decline to be ranked with either of them."[39] The two parties were, of course, the unorthodox and the separated evangelicals. The mixed multitude were those in alliance with the unorthodox. Of them, C. H. Spurgeon wrote: "In this army of intermediates are many who have no right to be there; but we spare them. The day will, however, come when they will have to reckon with their own consciences. When the light is taken out of its place they may have to mourn that they were not willing to trim the lamp, nor even to notice that the flame grew dim."[40]

He concluded with words that summarise his whole lonely battle for truth: "At any rate, cost what it may, to separate ourselves from those who separate themselves from the truth of God, is not alone our liberty, but our duty. I have raised my protest in the only complete way by coming forth and I shall be content to abide alone until the day when the Lord shall judge the secrets of all hearts; but it will not seem strange to me if others are found faithful, and if others judge that for them also there is no path but that which is painfully apart from the beaten track."[41]

References
1.   'The Sword and Trowel' March 1888 p. 147.
2.   ibid. pp. 121—127.
3.   ibid. pp. 148—150.
4.   ibid. p. 147.
5.   ibid. p. 147.
6.   ibid. pp. 147—148.
7.   ibid. p. 148.
8.   Quoted from Bacon, E. W. op. cit. p. 138.
9.   Bacon, E. W. op. cit. p. 139.
10.   'The Sword and Trowel' April 1888 pp. 157—160.
11.   ibid. p. 157.
12.   ibid. p. 159.
13.   ibid. p. 160.
14.   ibid. p. 160.
15.   ibid. p. 171.
16.   ibid. p. 198.
17.   'The Sword and Trowel' May 1888 p. 249.
18.   ibid. p. 249.
19.   ibid. pp. 204—208.
20.   ibid. p. 204.
21.   ibid. p. 205.

22. ibid. pp. 237—238.
23. 'The Sword and Trowel' June 1888 pp. 257—265, July 1888 pp. 337—345.
24. 'The Sword and Trowel' June 1888 p. 257.
25. 'The Sword and Trowel' July 1888 p. 343.
26. ibid. pp. 343—344.
27. Quoted Murray, I. op. cit. p. 218—219.
28. Bacon, E. W. op. cit. p. 139.
29. Quoted Murray, I. op. cit. p. 156.
30. Underwood, A. C. op. cit. p. 230.
31. Underwood, A. C. op. cit. p. 230.
32. "To whom it may concern" insert 29th April 1888 pp. 1—2.
33. ibid. p. 2.
34. Quoted Murray, I. op. cit. p. 154.
35. 'The Sword and Trowel' June 1888 p. 299.
36. ibid. p. 299.
37. ibid. p. 299.
38. 'The Sword and Trowel' December 1888 pp. 617—620.
39. ibid. p. 619.
40. ibid. p. 619.
41. ibid. p. 620.

9.
The 'Downgrade' continued and countered

As we turn from the nineteenth century to the
twentieth century, we are caused to ask whether the
situation has become better or worse. In C. H.
Spurgeon's day the main nonconformist bodies —
the Baptists, the Congregationalists and the Methodists — represented three stages of infiltration and
subjugation by unorthodoxy. C. H. Spurgeon's
opinion was that the Methodists were little affected
by unorthodoxy,[1] the Baptists were increasingly
affected[2] and the Congregationalists were well on
the road to unorthodoxy.[3]

The twentieth century saw the main denominations of these bodies in rapid theological decline,
leaving evangelicalism behind, or at least making
it a minority interest. K. S. Latourette stated: "In
the 1920s and 1930s English Congregationalism
seemed to be moving far in the direction of liberalism, minimising historic Christian doctrine and
stressing experience and the restating of the faith
in terms of the thought of the day."[4] He then
records a reaction against liberalism — but not an
evangelical one. Rather there was a turning to the
neo-orthodoxy of P. T. Forsyth and Karl Barth.[5]
Ultimately, unorthodox Congregationalism has been
swallowed up in the misnamed United Reformed
Church.

As for the Methodists, their decline from the

evangelical faith has been clear to see. Their most
famous "son", Lord Soper, recently gave an interview on his eightieth birthday in which he attacked
the revival of "Bible idolatry" by obscurantists (his
term for evangelicals), pinned his hopes for the
future of the nation on the "hard left" of the Labour
Party and surmised that he might one day experience
reincarnation![6]

Whereas K. S. Latourette (writing in the 1960s)
argued that in the early 1920s and 1930s Baptists
were not as committed as Congregationalists to
liberalism, nor later to neo-orthodoxy,[7] it must be
noted that Iain Murray writes of the prominent
Baptist T. R. Glover that he "spent a considerable
part of his life attempting an intellectual demolition
of historic Christianity" and that in 1932 he "gloried
in the fact that there were no colleges left adhering
to the position of the old evangelical confessions."[8]

In 1934, Henry Oakley, who had been at the
Baptist Union Assembly when C. H. Spurgeon's
views were rejected in April 1888 and who had
followed him out of the Union, wrote of the Baptist
Union: "The Baptist Union ceased to be a union of
likeminded men and churches, and became the union
of men and churches widely separated in faith and
practice — a kind of theological Woolworth's, where
variety is the principal thing. All that Mr. Spurgeon
saw, and much more had come to pass."[9]

Since the Second World War things have not
changed. The real triumph of unorthodoxy in the
Baptist Union was seen when Principal Michael
Taylor of the Northern Baptist College denied the
deity of Christ at the Baptist Union Assembly in

1971. The consequent furore resulted in another
paper compromise like that of 1888, whereby Mr.
Taylor's blasphemous views were permissible in the
Union and he remained undisciplined. Indeed, to
some he became a sort of folk-hero, and still pro-
motes heresies.

The comprehensiveness that C. H. Spurgeon saw
in the Church of England of his day and condemned[10] has now become a reality in the Free
Churches. Evangelicalism co-exists with unorthodoxy
in the main-line denominations and is, therefore,
open to exactly the same challenges that C. H.
Spurgeon gave in his day. Unorthodoxy is no longer
stealthily infiltrating under a mask of evangelicalism.
It is dominant. The issue, therefore, is clear. As
unorthodoxy is proven beyond all doubt to be a
considerable, and even dominant, force in the Church
of England, the United Reformed Church, the
Methodist Church, the Baptist Union and various
similar bodies, is it biblically permissible for evangelicals to remain in these bodies? C. H. Spurgeon's
answer is clear: "fellowship with known and vital
error is participation in sin."[11] The duty of evangelicals is obvious. Those who fellowship with the
unorthodox involve themselves in their wickedness
(2 John 10—11). Guilt by association is a biblical
doctrine. Separation from error is mandatory —
a divine requirement on the believer.

The change in position on the part of the Evangelical Alliance must also be noted. In 1888 C. H.
Spurgeon looked upon the Alliance as doing "grand
service to the cause of truth" and spoke warmly of
its reception and support of him.[12] Over the years

the Alliance has come to represent those who have stayed in apostate denominations, whose philosophy is 'in it to win it'. It is an anti-separatist body.

In an article in 'The Life of Faith', the former chairman of the Evangelical Alliance, the Rev. G. W. Kirby, lamented the emphasis on separatism which was made in the late 1960s by the Rev. Dr. M. Lloyd-Jones (to whom we shall return later). He reviewed the first half of the twentieth century when "our various evangelical societies enjoyed equally the support of Christians linked with the historic denominations as well as those independent of them".[13]

Mr. Kirby explained that many felt they should stay in the mixed denominations "until they are forced out, or until their freedom to preach the Gospel as they understand it is impaired . . . They claim a right to remain in their denominations because the historic position of those denominations has not been officially repudiated".[14]

He then explained the separatist position: "This position is strongly assailed by those 'separatists' who feel that a Christian minister is seriously compromised by remaining in a denomination which countenances those who have seriously departed from a Biblical faith, and who in some cases openly repudiate such a faith".[15]

Mr. Kirby's confessions are amazing! He recognises that by the late 1960s the historic denominations were not simply being infiltrated by the unorthodox, as in C. H. Spurgeon's day, but that they countenanced those "who have seriously departed from a Biblical faith and who in some

cases openly repudiate such a faith"! The day had
arrived which C. H. Spurgeon predicted when the
unorthodox would be tolerated in nonconformity
as part of comprehensive denominations.[16]

Mr. Kirby's tactics in the light of this also need
to be given emphasis. Evangelicals, he argued,
should stay in alliance with those who depart from
and repudiate the biblical faith until such time as
the denomination officially repudiates evangelicalism, excludes evangelicals or silences them! Such
arguments show a complete failure to understand
the tactics of unorthodoxy in history. Unorthodoxy
makes its advance in the face of tolerance and under-
mines orthodoxy like a slowly creeping paralysis.
It does not need to repudiate evangelicalism ex-
plicitly because it constantly destroys and overthrows
it by more subtle means. Unorthodoxy is always
happy to keep evangelical terminology because it
simply redefines the terms and makes them meaningless. When words can mean anything they mean
nothing.

Mr. Kirby has also correctly understood the
separatist position. Men who are willing to be in
fellowship with others who seriously depart from
a biblical faith and openly repudiate it are compromised; and more than that, they are sinning.
To such men, C. H. Spurgeon said: "Numbers of
good brethren in different ways remain in fellowship with those who are undermining the gospel;
and they talk of their conduct as though it were a
loving course which the Lord will approve of in the
day of his appearing. We cannot understand them.
The bounden duty of a true believer towards men

who profess to be Christians, and yet deny the Word of the Lord and reject the fundamentals of the gospel, is to come out from among them."[17]

The question that remains is: were there none who followed C. H. Spurgeon's separatist position, and, if there were, what has happened to them?

As we have seen, a few men and churches left the Baptist Union in support of C. H. Spurgeon. Some of these met and composed a confession of faith as the basis of their unity together which was evangelical, Calvinistic and premillenial. Its most important clause was the first, which was a rebuttal of the Higher Critical view of scripture. "We, the undersigned, banded together in Fraternal Union, observing with growing pain and sorrow the loosening hold of many upon the Truths of Revelation, are constrained to avow our firmest belief in the Verbal Inspiration of all Holy Scripture as originally given. To us, the Bible does not merely contain the Word of God but *is* the Word of God. From beginning to end, we accept it, believe it and continue to preach it. To us, the Old Testament is no less inspired than the New. The Book is an organic whole. Reverence for the NEW Testament accompanied by scepticism as to the OLD appears to us absurd. The two must stand or fall together. We accept Christ's own verdict concerning 'Moses and all the prophets' in preference to any supposed discoveries of so-called Higher Criticism".[18]

The general attitude of others to this small group of men and their confession of faith was one of patronising condescension. They were seen as the last representatives of a dying theology which could not come to terms with the "advances" made by "modern thought".

With the death of C. H. Spurgeon in 1892, his small band of supporters continued, but usually in a policy of rigid independence — even isolationism. When attempts were made in the 1920s to draw independent separatist congregations together in the 'Fellowship of Undenominational and Unattached Churches and Missions' (later the Fellowship of Independent Evangelical Churches), some of these men were forthright in their opposition. They had tested the tendency to corruption in formal union and hesitated to be bound up in it again.[19]

Mention of the Fellowship of Independent Evangelical Churches (FIEC) is necessary and important at this point because its instigator, E. J. Poole-Connor, was a solidly Spurgeonic man. He was a staunch opponent of modernism and an unreserved supporter of the stand C. H. Spurgeon had taken. He maintained his negative teaching on separation from heresy and developed his positive teaching on evangelical unity. It was out of these convictions that the FIEC was formed.

The sort of separation advocated by E. J. Poole-Connor and foundational to the ethos of the FIEC as originally envisaged may be seen from the following quotation from E. J. Poole-Connor's book "The Apostasy of English Nonconformists" (1933). In his introduction he says: "One of the most disquieting features of the present religious situation in England is the attitude of Conservative Evangelical Nonconformists towards the form of teaching known as Modernism.

"In view of their historic claim to speak their minds freely it would have been thought impossible that they should permit their denominational leaders to foster principles that are so largely the negation of the older faith without some vigorous protest. Equally difficult would it have been to believe that they could, with apparent cordiality, co-operate with those who not only controvert their most cherished convictions, but often do so in terms of obloquy and derision.

"Yet the majority of Evangelicals associated with The Free Churches seem to be able to do both. Neither the partiality of their leaders for liberal theology nor the contumely heaped upon their own beliefs appear to strain their allegiance. The ecclesiastical machinery runs as smoothly as ever."[20]

E. J. Poole-Connor's reason for opposing the quiet indifference shown to unorthodoxy by the evangelicals in the main denominations was not left without explanation. He wrote: "It need scarcely be said that this attitude constitutes a very real danger to the Evangelical cause. It can only be construed by the rising generation, for example, in one of two ways. Either they will believe that those who profess the older faith hold it so lightly, that it is to them a matter of indifference whether the contrary doctrines are taught or not; or else that there is so little essential difference between the two that their divergence is mainly a question of terminology. They will conclude that in either case nothing really matters."[21]

But E. J. Poole-Connor realised that the failure to speak out and separate from error not only made

light of that error in the present but also condemned
the past history of separatism. "For issues not one
whit more serious than those which faced the Evangelicals of today their forefathers surrendered almost
all they held most dear, and went out not knowing
whither they went."[22]

E. J. Poole-Connor believed that separation from
the unorthodox was necessary. He knew that
separatism was often accused of being isolationist
but he defended himself and those of like mind in
the FIEC from such a charge. "There are many who
have no love of isolation; no desire — God is witness — to separate from fellow-believers. They realise
how good and pleasant it is for brethren to dwell
together in unity; not only because such unity is
essentially Christian, but also because of its value
in testimony to the world without. Nevertheless so
gravely do they regard the present departure from
the faith that they have felt compelled to sever themselves from associations in which they were born and
bred, and with which some of their dearest memories
are intertwined. Have they done so without reason?
Have they magnified minor divergencies into serious
apostasies? They think not. They feel that the
changes are in the realm of vital things, things concerning which they must at all cost, keep their
conscience clear."[23]

There can be no doubt that these quotations prove
E. J. Poole-Connor to have been thoroughly
Spurgeonic. He believed in the necessity of protest
against and separation from unorthodoxy. But he
also shared C. H. Spurgeon's hope of the unity of
evangelicals. But unlike C. H. Spurgeon, who saw it

as a hope for the future, E. J. Poole-Connor sought to realise it in the present in the FIEC. He recognised with C. H. Spurgeon that the major denominations agreed on lesser matters (e.g. belief in baptism by immersion is essential to membership of the Baptist Union), but disagreed on the greater (e.g. belief in the deity of Christ varies in the Baptist Union!) He desired to form a separatist fellowship with agreement on the fundamentals of the faith but allowing variation on the interpretation of scripture in relation to lesser matters. To use his words, "Let the bond of union henceforth be the great verities of the evangelical faith and let the liberty of individual conviction be in regard to the lesser issues."[24] The great principle at the centre of the FIEC was freedom of interpretation in non-fundamentals but "the preservation of the evangelical faith" as the "chief concern".[25]

In the formation of the FIEC and its development, E. J. Poole-Connor went beyond C. H. Spurgeon. C. H. Spurgeon had looked for an informal alliance and had seen this developing only in the context of prayer and greater study of the Word. E. J. Poole-Connor created a formal alliance based upon the affirmation of separatist principles with regard to modernism and evangelical beliefs.

In 1952 E. J. Poole-Connor realised that there were other church groupings which opposed unorthodoxy, were separate from it and were committed to the evangelical faith. He was therefore involved in forming the British Evangelical Council (BEC), which initially included the FIEC, the Free Church of Scotland and the Evangelical Presbyterian Church of Northern Ireland.

Unlike the FIEC, the British Evangelical Council was not a fellowship of individual congregations, but a council of evangelical church groupings. These groupings were joined together on the basis of a common doctrinal statement of evangelical fundamentals. They are described in BEC literature as "one on the fundamental doctrines of the faith", as desiring "to discover and experience that true ecumenicity which the Scriptures clearly teach" and as "united in their opposition to that form of unscriptural ecumenicity represented by the World Council of Churches".[26]

In these statements the heritage passed on from C. H. Spurgeon is clearly seen. There is a commitment to evangelical fundamentals, a rejection of unity with those who deny the fundamentals, and a desire to seek unity with those who maintain the fundamentals.

The policy of the British Evangelical Council has been set out in various documents and publications. Perhaps the most notable sermon ever preached at a BEC meeting was "Luther and his message for today" by Dr. D. M. Lloyd-Jones in 1967.

Prior to the meeting Dr. Lloyd-Jones had created considerable trouble by asserting separatist principles. His evangelical Anglican colleagues in particular had taken great exception to his public pronouncements and a variety of meetings, including the Puritan Conference and the Westminster Fellowship, had been dissolved and reconstituted on separatist principles.

In his BEC sermon, Dr. Lloyd-Jones attacked the compromise formulas with double meanings which satisfied the evangelicals and the unorthodox. "Everybody can accept the formula, the magic formula, though they interpret it in diametrically opposed ways . . . They have got a marvellous formula: and though two groups are fundamentally opposed in their doctrine it satisfies both sides and so they achieve 'unity'".[27] This was precisely what C. H. Spurgeon rejected in the Baptist Union statement of faith.

He then turned to the idea of association with the unorthodox and issued statements that are thoroughly Spurgeonic in character. "To a man who has his only authority in the Scriptures there is no possible compromise with, first of all, the Church of Rome . . . But not only is compromise with such people impossible for the Evangelical, it is equally impossible for him to be yoked together with others in the Church who deny the very elements of the Christian faith."[28]

Echoing C. H. Spurgeon's assertion that "fellowship with known and vital error is participation in sin", Dr. Lloyd-Jones stated, "It also raises the question of guilt by association. If you are content to function in the same church with such people — the two groups I have mentioned — you are virtually saying that though you think you are right, they also may be right, and this is a possible interpretation of Scripture. That, I assert, is a denial of the Evangelical, the only true, faith. It is impossible."[29]

Like C. H. Spurgeon, Dr. Lloyd-Jones also rejected the idea of remaining in denominations to win them back to an evangelical faith — the 'in it to win it' philosophy. He said, "The idea that Evangelicals

can infiltrate any established church — above all,
the Church of Rome — and reform it, and turn it
into an Evangelical body, is midsummer madness.
No institution has ever been truly reformed. The
Puritan movement and 1662 bear eloquent testimony to that fact. This is the verdict of history."[30]

He concluded his address with a call to separation
and to formal unity. "What then are we as Evangelicals to do in this situation? I reply by saying
that we must heed a great injunction in Revelation
18:4, 'Come out of her, my people! Come out of
her, my people, that ye be not partakers of her
sins, and that ye receive not of her plagues.' Come
out of it! But come together also, come into fellowship with all like-minded Christian people. Come
into an association such as this British Evangelical
Council, that stands for the truth and against compromise, hesitation, neutrality, and everything that
but ministers to the success of the plans of Rome
and the Ecumenical Movement. Come out; come
in!"[31]

Dr. Lloyd-Jones and C. H. Spurgeon both used
the "Come out of Babylon" motif in their argument
but like E. J. Poole-Connor, Dr. Lloyd-Jones saw
the formal alliance of the BEC as the way ahead and,
therefore, committed himself to this alliance of
church groupings.

Soon after the 1967 BEC Conference the statement "BEC Attitude to Ecumenicity" was published.
This was prepared in January 1968 and then published and deserves attention as the official position
of the BEC allied churches, viz. FIEC, the Evangelical
Presbyterian Church of Northern Ireland, the three

Strict Baptist Associations, the Free Church of Scotland, the Evangelical Movement of Wales, the Evangelical Fellowship of Congregational Churches, the Union of Evangelical Churches and the Apostolic Church. Whilst some of these church groupings were not in membership with the BEC in 1968, by joining it since they have implicitly affirmed their acceptance of its official policy.

The pamphlet is particularly related to the World Council of Churches and the type of ecumenicity it represents, i.e. the comprehensive view of unity — orthodox and unorthodox fellowshipping together. The main principles of the pamphlet are:

1. To remain in doctrinally mixed denominations "is contrary to scriptural principles" because "thereby (1) the Gospel is compromised if not denied since such is an attempt to achieve organisational union at the expense of vital Christian truths"[32] and "(2) real evangelical unity is hindered."

2. Having attacked the comprehensive nature of the World Council of Churches, the pamphlet states, "For ourselves we cannot be associated in any way with a movement which implies that the evangelical position is but one of many insights or traditions and which necessarily requires evangelical churches, directly or indirectly associated with it, to be in fellowship as fellow-Christian churches with religious bodies which do not hold to the very essentials of biblical Christianity . . . We believe evangelical churches ought to be seen in fellowship with each other and not with those who reject the authority of Scripture and the complete work of Christ."[33]

3. The pamphlet looks forward to evangelical unity

at church level and sees the alliance of groups of
churches as a step to this end. The two principles
of active dissociation from unorthodoxy and
uncompromised fellowship together are reiterated.

4. Recognising that some would argue (for
example, the Evangelical Alliance) that differing
attitudes to the Ecumenical Movement should not
cause division amongst true brethren, the pamphlet
responds, "What is at stake is no mere interpretation
of Scripture but the Gospel itself. We totally reject
the plea that the issues raised are secondary matters.
They concern the very nature, purity and defence of
the Gospel itself . . . Scriptural justification can no
longer be found even for neutrality toward it, let
alone active participation in it."[34]

The importance of this fourth principle cannot
be overstated. The uncompromised evangelical is
in opposition to the compromised and views the
compromised evangelical in his alliance with the
unorthodox as sinful. The principle termed by
C. H. Spurgeon as "participation in sin", by D. M.
Lloyd-Jones as "guilt by association" and by the
Bible as "sharing in wickedness" (II John 11) is
affirmed as a necessary consequence of believing and
obeying Scripture.

5. The pamphlet recognised that it would take
some men a little time to extract themselves from
their compromised alliances. It assured them of a
warm welcome as they proceeded along the path
of dissociation from unorthodoxy.

6. The pamphlet asserts the desirability of retain-
ing personal fellowship with the compromised evangelical but not church fellowship.

We see then that the official position of the BEC

affiliated churches is one of separation from error
and also evangelical unity. It is avowedly part of
the Spurgeonic and biblical tradition.

References
1.   'The Sword and Trowel' April 1887, p. 195.
2.   'The Sword and Trowel' March 1887, p. 122. May 1888, p. 249.
3.   'The Sword and Trowel' July 1888, p. 379. August 1888,
     pp. 445–446.
4.   Latourette, K. S. (1961) *Christianity in the Revolutionary Age,*
     Vol. 4, Paternoster Press, p. 445.
5.   Latourette, K. S. op. cit. p. 446.
6.   Newsstand of the Methodist Church. Spring 1983.
7.   Latourette, K. S. op. cit. p. 446.
8.   Murray, I. op. cit. p. 163.
9.   Quoted Murray, I. op. cit. p. 163.
10. See Murray, I. op. cit. p. 143.
11. 'The Sword and Trowel' November 1887, p. 559.
12. 'The Sword and Trowel' May 1888, p. 249.
13. 'The Life of Faith' Thursday, 25th January 1968, p. 1.
14. ibid. p. 1.
15. ibid. p. 1.
16. 'The Sword and Trowel' January 1888, p. 44.
17. 'The Sword and Trowel' October 1888, p. 562.
18. Quoted Murray, I. op. cit. pp. 219–220.
19. Fountain, D. G. (1966) *"E. J. Poole-Connor"* Henry E. Walter,
     p. 124.
20. ibid. pp. 131–132.
21. ibid. p. 132.
22. ibid. p. 132.
23. ibid. p. 133.
24. ibid. p. 172.
25. ibid. p. 172.
26. Quoted from the Introductory form to the BEC.
27. Lloyd-Jones, D. M. (1968) *Luther and his message for today.*
     Evangelical Press, pp. 22–23.
28. ibid. p. 24.
29. ibid. p. 24–25.
30. ibid. pp. 26–27.
31. ibid. p. 27.
32. BEC Attitude to Ecumenicity (1968), p. 1.
33. ibid. pp. 1–2.
34. ibid. p. 2.

10.
C. H. Spurgeon and his heirs

The Downgrade Controversy raised questions which
are as important in the 1980s as they were in the
1880s. Four issues in particular need consideration:
The attitude of C. H. Spurgeon and his heirs to:

1. Those who deny the fundamentals of the faith.
2. Those in alliance with those who deny the
fundamentals.
3. Those differences between evangelicals which
are not fundamental.
4. Evangelical unity.

1. Those who deny the fundamentals of the faith
In relation to their separation from those who deny
the fundamentals of the faith, C. H. Spurgeon has had
many heirs over the last one hundred years. Although
they used different terminology, E. J. Poole-Connor
and Dr. D. M. Lloyd-Jones and those churches and
church groupings associated with them in the FIEC
and BEC (not forgetting some completely independent churches) all affirmed that "fellowship with
known and vital error is participation in sin".[1]
Fellowship with modernists and Catholics was
shunned.

From amongst the separatists, however, new
voices have arisen over the past few years. Whereas
the ecumenical movement in its structural, ecclesiastical form had little attraction for separatist

churches and was an easy prey to their vociferous attacks, two modern movements have caused some to abandon Spurgeonic (i.e. biblical) principles of separation from those who deny the fundamentals of the faith. These two movements are "crusade evangelism" and the "charismatic movement".

It is easy to see why separatist evangelicals are willing to sell their birthright for the sake of evangelism. The preaching of the gospel is the very "bread and butter" of evangelical life. Any attempt to make Christ known has a magnetic attraction for the evangelical. When evangelism is mentioned both pulpit and pew are interested and enthused. "Will the constant cry for conversions now be heard?" it is asked.

Whereas in the early 1950s the crusades of Billy Graham attracted some separatist support because the gospel was being preached and the support came seemingly from evangelicals, by the 1960s the crusade machinery and platform parties in Britain were Anglican dominated and not exclusively evangelical. This trend was defended by Dr. R. O. Ferm in his book "Co-operative Evangelism: Is Billy Graham Right or Wrong?".[2] This alliance with modernists alarmed many separatists and called forth a number of books and considerable opposition. Generally, evangelical separatists withdrew from too much involvement with Billy Graham, for co-operation with him meant fellowship with those who denied the fundamentals.

Co-operation with "such convinced and unrepentant Modernists as Dr. G. F. Fisher, Bishop Mervyn Stockwood, Dr. John Sutherland Bonnell, Bishop

James Pike, Henry Van Dusen, Bishop Gerald Kennedy, Dr. Robert Schuller, and a host of others" has gone hand-in-hand with "increasing involvement with Roman Catholicism".[3]

Dr. Graham has tolerated Roman Catholic involvement in his campaign since at least 1972 and has actively encouraged Roman Catholics to stay in their church, pleading, "Above all, don't pull out of the Church". Roman Catholic converts are fed back into the Roman Catholic church in some of the crusades.[4] In the first half of 1984 the national and religious press reported hundreds at mass in support of Billy Graham and a pilgrimage to the shrine of Mary at Walsingham on his behalf.

Although the degree of Catholic and modernist involvement in Mission England varied from area to area, it was undoubtedly an ecumenical venture. John Williamson, the Regional Co-ordinator for Mission England in the North West, wrote: "Mission England is not and must not be limited to support from evangelical churches".[5]

Mission England is not, therefore, a problem to evangelicals because they are not sure whether "Billy Graham is a Christian",[6] as some misleadingly claim. The spiritual standing of Billy Graham is not the issue. The real difficulty arises because involvement meant association for religious purposes with people who hold to another gospel: in some cases a Roman Catholic gospel, in others a modernistic gospel.

How then has the FIEC as a separatist organisation responded to Mission England? In its official broadsheet sent to all its member churches the heirs of

E. J. Poole-Connor wrote, "Some people have asked 'What is the FIEC attitude to Mission England?' The answer is that there is no official attitude."

To explain this sudden nullification of its separatist roots and heritage, the FIEC office claims the FIEC is not a denomination and it must not interfere with independent churches. It stated four views held in the FIEC churches with regard to Mission England: *1.* Enthusiastic and total commitment. Such churches, we are told, see that there "are some snags in co-operation"; *2.* Limited commitment; *3.* Prayerful concern without official co-operation. Under this heading Roman Catholic involvement is recognised and the complete absence of a doctrinal basis stated; *4.* Total dissociation. The list is followed with a plea, "We must not allow this issue to divide us".[7]

In a published response to FIEC news, Rev. T. O. Jenkins wrote that whereas the FIEC had rightly eschewed denominationalism, "this surely has not precluded leadership, clear witness and firm pronouncements when required so that its member churches, though independent, should not be left to flounder in the religious morass of the day".[8] The Metropolitan Association of Strict Baptist Churches did precisely this in a document (not a directive) it issued to its constituency on ecumenical evangelistic efforts. The FIEC could have acted similarly but preferred to adopt no position of guidance and leadership.

Perhaps C. H. Spurgeon's ironical comments are as applicable to the statements of the FIEC as to the BU of his day. In writing of their diplomatic non-stance he wrote, "We cannot help it, but in reading these carefully prepared epistles, there has passed before our mind the vision of the heroic Nelson, with the telescope at his blind eye, and we have heard him say again and again, 'I cannot see it'. With a brave blindness he refused to see that which might have silenced his guns. Brethren who have been officials of a denomination have a paternal partiality about them which is so natural, and so sacred, that we have not the heart to censure it. Above all things, these prudent brethren feel bound to preserve the prestige of the body and the peace of the committee."[9]

The second great influence on separatists that has encouraged a looser attitude towards fellowship with modernists and Roman Catholics is the charismatic movement.

Initially, the charismatic movement began to spread across the mainline denominations. "Denominational barriers began to fall. Speaking with tongues became the experience of Episcopalians, Orthodox, Presbyterians, Baptists, Lutherans".[10] "Thus we began to read about a Spirit-filled Baptist, a Spirit-filled Methodist, a Spirit-filled Lutheran and so on. Through this means the Holy Spirit emphasis became a part of the ecumenical stream."[11]

It was not long, however, before the non-evangelical segments of the mainline denominations began to be affected, as the following incident makes clear. "When the neo-Pentecostal movement was getting under way in the Los Angeles area in the 1960s I talked to an Assembly of God preacher about the phenomenon. He said 'We used to be the leaders in experiencing the baptism in the Holy Spirit but not since the Spirit has visited the great historic and Protestant churches.' I know an Episcopalian priest in this city who is so liberal he neither believes in the virgin birth nor the resurrection. Yet he has recently received the baptism in the Spirit." [12]

I am in contact with an Anglo-Catholic priest who delights in Mariolatry, rejects the necessity of conversion for everyone, and holds to many further opportunities after death for the acceptance of salvation. He too is a charismatic!

Not only modernists and Anglo-Catholics share a common charismatic experience, but Roman Catholics also. Whilst some Roman Catholics experience true conversion and a charismatic experience and leave the Church of Rome, others are simply confirmed in the errors of their Catholicism by it. Let a Roman Catholic monk confirm this. "The experience of the Pentecostal Movement tends to confirm the validity and relevance of our authentic spiritual traditions." [13] Or elsewhere in his other writings, "Similarly, the traditional devotions of the Church have taken on more meaning. Some people have been brought back to a frequent use of the sacrament of Penance through the experience of the baptism in the Spirit. Others have discovered a place for devotion to Mary in their lives, whereas previously they had been indifferent or even antipathetic toward her. One of the most striking effects of the Holy Spirit's action has been to stir up devotion to the Real Presence in the Eucharist." [14]

Alongside modernist, Anglo-Catholic and Roman Catholic charismatics, the charismatic movement has

also affected the sects. Robert Brinsmead reported
an invitation he had received to address Pentecostal
Christadelphians who denied the divinity of Christ,
his pre-existence before Bethlehem, the personality
of the Holy Spirit, etc.[15] Yet they claimed the
same charismatic experience as others.

Many of the questions raised by the charismatic
movement are outside the scope of this book. The
issue to which this section of this chapter is
addressed is our attitude to fellowship with those
who deny the fundamentals of the faith. As there
are signs that some who claim to be separatists are
in association with those who deny the fundamentals
because of a common charismatic experience, it is
necessary to sound an alarm lest "gifts" become the
Trojan Horse by which heretical ecumenicity infil-
trates separatist churches and bodies. As gifts are
not even an evidence of the possession of salvation
(Matthew 7:21–23, cf. Judas Iscariot, Balaam) and
as there is an experience of the Spirit which a man
can have yet which does not prevent apostasy
(Hebrews 6:4–6), a common experience of "the
Spirit and his gifts" is no basis for fellowship. Whatever spiritual gifting may be claimed, if apostolic
doctrine is not acknowledged the gifted are to be
ignored (I Corinthians 14:37–38).

2. Those in alliance with those who deny the funda-
   mentals

Over the last hundred years separatists have con-
sistently argued the case for separation from those
who deny the fundamentals and have severed their
alliances with them. Ecumenical relations with

modernists and Roman Catholics have, therefore, been non-existent. However, there has also existed a group (often large) of evangelicals who whilst rejecting modernism and Catholicism nevertheless maintain official and fellowship links with them in denominations, fraternals, committees, movements and special events.

In the 'Downgrade' controversy, as we have seen, few of C. H. Spurgeon's fellow Baptists in the Union were willing to speak out and separate from the modernists as he did. The great mass of the evangelicals remained compromised in the alliance of the Union. We need to trace C. H. Spurgeon's attitude to his compromised brethren before his secession and after it.

When C. H. Spurgeon personally entered the attack on the modernists in the Union he quickly noticed the presence of those who accepted any man whatever his views as long as he was clever and good-natured. He regretted this tendency, and discouraged any policy of silence in the face of error on the part of evangelicals.[16]

Month by month his annoyance and frustration with those evangelicals who wished to be evangelical yet not speak out against error increased. He accused them of "fear" and "shrinking" from their duty and of being "tame",[17] of "dreaming".[18] As secession drew near for him he stated his hope that non-seceders would have weighty reasons to justify their actions and not be acting treasonably. He affirmed his love for them but not for their alliances.[19]

The theme of treasonable alliances became stronger

as C. H. Spurgeon recognised the inevitable need
of resignation from the Union if he would avoid
sin through fellowship with error.[20] Whilst considering those in the Union wrong, however, he
did not break fellowship with them. In his letter
to Dr. Culross he wrote: "Do I need to say that,
with you, and such brethren as Dr. McLaren, Mr.
Aldis and Dr. Angus, I have no sort of disagreement,
except that you stay in the Union and I am out of
it? We shall, according to our light, labour for the
same cause. We are all Christians and Baptists, and
can find many ways of co-operation." Having stated
that he could not fellowship with them in the Union,
he continued, "we are not therefore deprived of a
thousand other ways of fellowship. You feel union
of heart with men who publicly preach Universal
Restitution: I do not. I mean, you feel enough fellowship to remain in the Union with them: I do not. It is
the same with other errors. Still, I am in fellowship
with you — Union or no Union."[21]

One of the main reasons why C. H. Spurgeon did
not break fellowship with those who stayed in
the Union was because he recognised that there
were faithful brethren who were trying to win the
Union for evangelicalism. He saw this as sincere
but futile. However, he recognised that if the day
came when modernists were to be allowed in the
Union, i.e. if an evangelical basis for the Union
was rejected, then such brethren would have to
secede.[22] He could sympathise with men fighting
a last ditch stand but not with those who would
then surrender to the new order of a comprehensive
Union.

It is important to pause at this point and note the complete misunderstanding of C. H. Spurgeon's position and that of the separatists who followed him. C. H. Spurgeon was not opposed to a man fighting modernist infiltration in his denomination. Rather, he fully supported it. However, when those men lost the will to fight and ceased to attack modernism, gave up polemics and acquiesced in paper compromise, he condemned it. When the evangelical group in a denomination had lost the battle and the modernists were in control, C. H. Spurgeon believed it to be a biblical duty to secede. C. H. Spurgeon did not argue that a man's first duty when faced with error was to secede, but he did insist that when the battle was lost and the modernists had won the right to remain or had taken over the denomination, secession was a necessary duty.

C. H. Spurgeon's position (that if the evangelicals lost the battle to keep those in error out of their denominations they had to secede) is reflected in his comments on Bishop J. C. Ryle. Whereas some claim "J. C. Ryle, still within Anglicanism, but pointing away from Puseyism to 'the old paths', is not guilty by association".[23] C. H. Spurgeon stated of J. C. Ryle's papers on Church Principles and Church Comprehensiveness, "There is no party within the Church of England with whom we are more nearly agreed than the Evangelical, and yet they excite more our wonder and pity than our sympathy. We wonder they are not ashamed of being connected with men who openly defy the law and preach the worst form of Popery. We pity them because, while they remain in the Establishment, their protests against its errors have but little power. The writer of the present papers is an evangelical champion, for whom we entertain a profound regard. The first of his papers is a strong protest against the superstitious practices of the Anglicans: but yet in the second paper he pleads hard for a comprehension which shall include believers in doctrines which are diametrically opposed to each other. Such is the sad influence of a false position. One of the bravest and best of men is found temporizing in a way which grieves thousands even in his own denomination. Congresses in which Christ and antichrist are brought together cannot but exercise a very unhealthy influence even upon the most decided followers of truth. We wish Mr. Ryle could review his own position in the light of the Scriptures rather than in the darkness of ecclesiasticism: then would he come out from among them, and no more touch the unclean thing."[24]

When the Union ultimately adopted its paper compromise, C. H. Spurgeon found himself out on a limb with even his own brother seeing the compromise as a victory. He refused to accuse his brother of bad motives but felt compelled to differ in his estimate of the usefulness of the new creed. He recognised that few would now see the reason for separation.

By October 1888, as more and more evidence was amassed, C. H. Spurgeon felt it necessary to write at length of the brethren who stayed in the mixed denominations. "Every day affords more and more evidence that while many are true to the Lord, unbelief has sadly eaten into Congregational and Baptist Churches . . . The door is open, and droves of falsehoods enter by it. Numbers of good brethren in different ways remain in fellowship with those who are undermining the gospel, and they talk of their conduct as though it were a loving course which the Lord will approve of in the day of his appearing. We cannot understand them. The bounden duty of a true believer towards men who profess to be Christians and yet deny the Word of the Lord and reject the fundamentals of the gospel is to come out from among them."[25]

Knowing that many would argue that they were staying in the Union to reform it, C. H. Spurgeon argued that the basis of the Union allowed error and prevented reform. Evangelical parties in mixed bodies merely hid the true problem instead of standing apart, and involved themselves in sinful compromise and inevitable decline. They were the very cover under which heresy stealthily advanced. Again he pleaded for separation.[26]

In the final years of his life, C. H. Spurgeon continued occasionally to fire broadsides at the brethren in the Union who lived in a world of sleepiness and pretence, declaring all was well.[27] He attacked them for shortsightedness, treachery and treason[28] and continued to amass his evidence.[29]

We are now in a position to summarise C. H. Spurgeon's attitude to those in alliance with men who denied the fundamentals of the faith. He considered them to be acting sinfully and treasonably. Nevertheless he accepted that they were evangelicals and that fellowship with them was permissible. In having fellowship with them in various ways he did

not leave them without regular rebuke for their
alliances. The relationship must have been somewhat
strained, for in no sense did C. H. Spurgeon agree to
disagree and leave the matter alone. He disagreed
vocally and clearly and retained his strongest links
with the men who held his position fully. He kept
his church free of official alliances but had personal
fraternal links with some of the compromised
brethren.

The heirs of C. H. Spurgeon have followed his
lead to varying degrees. As we have seen, until
recently considerable care was taken over keeping
separate from Catholicism and modernism. Also,
fellowship links that did not involve alliance with
those who denied the fundamentals were retained.
In the 1950s and early 1960s, therefore, separatist
churches and evangelical churches within the denominations were in close fellowship in the support of
various activities. As G. W. Kirby correctly said,
"Our various evangelical societies enjoyed equally
the support of Christians linked with the historic
denominations as well as those independent of
them".[30] In evangelical societies churches of the
Evangelical Alliance ethos and the British Evangelical Council ethos met together.

The fundamental difference between the relationship of C. H. Spurgeon and the compromised
brethren and the evangelical scene of the 1950s and
early 1960s was that the voice of separatist criticism
had virtually ceased. The separatist churches lacked
Spurgeonic polemics. There was little condemnation
of compromise and little call for secession. Separatists and non-separatists allowed harmony to continue

and no objections to be raised. E. J. Poole-Connor had died and no-one had taken up a militant separatist stance.

In this climate of uncritical brotherhood the idea was mooted that a National Association of Evangelicals should be formed. The minister of Westminster Chapel, Dr. D. M. Lloyd-Jones, refused to join it. He was invited to speak to a large gathering of evangelicals at the Westminster Central Hall. He was given a "carte blanche" and at that meeting raised the issue of secession from those denominations which were comprehensive as a first step to true evangelical unity.

The voice of C. H. Spurgeon was heard again. The comfortable indifference to alliances with those who denied the fundamentals was shattered. Union after secession was the call. The chairman, an Anglican evangelical, stood to dissociate himself from what had been said and totally to disagreee.[31] The issue of secession had again been raised and was to transform evangelical patterns of fellowship.

The call to secession from mixed denominations issued by Dr. Lloyd-Jones had widespread repercussions. The year 1967 saw four significant events. The Puritan Conference, of which Dr. Lloyd-Jones was the chairman, closed. The men who wished to remain in compromised positions in mixed denominations were excluded[32] from the committee and a new separatist committee was formed to call a reconstituted conference entitled the Westminster Conference.

Dr. Lloyd-Jones' own fraternal, the Westminster Fellowship, was thrown into turmoil over the issue

of secession. It was also closed down and the brethren
who would not commit themselves to secession from
the mixed denominations were excluded when it
was reconstituted.

The other significant events in 1967 were two
conferences representing very different constituencies
and reaching diametrically opposed conclusions. The
first of these conferences was an assembly of evangelical Anglicans at Keele. Until that conference the
traditional view of evangelicals within the Church
of England had been that their church was officially
and constitutionally evangelical and that modernism
and Catholicism were hybrid, enemy incursions into
the church which ought to be opposed. At Keele,
however, the Anglican evangelicals "pledged themselves to adopt a new attitude in which they would
regard the *whole* Church of England a valid church
in the favour of God".[33] The centuries-old view of
evangelicals as the true heirs of the Church of
England constitution was abandoned for a comprehensive church of equals. From that time on evangelicalism was to be seen as one viewpoint amongst
Anglicans, and modernism and Catholicism were
others. Evangelicalism was no longer seen as the
only legitimate form of Anglicanism.

The other conference, which has already been
referred to at some length in an earlier chapter, was
the British Evangelical Council Conference of 1967
which culminated in the "Luther Rally". There, in
the clearest possible terms, Dr. Lloyd-Jones gave
his call for secession and the unity of the seceders.[34]
The call to secession was as clear-cut as anything
ever said by C. H. Spurgeon.

Like C. H. Spurgeon, Dr. Lloyd-Jones did not
sever all fellowship with compromised evangelicals.
He respected those who vocally opposed error within
their denominations although he believed them
wrong not to secede. He respected the problems of
those who took time over their secession, as he
wanted them to bring their churches with them.
He even encouraged some men to go into churches
in mixed denominations if those churches were
looking for leadership and were able to be taught
the principles of secession. He was certainly willing
to preach for men in mixed denominations. His
policy could be summarised in the phrases "brother-
liness without approval" or "limited fellowship".

The policies of no fellowship with modernists
and Catholics and limited fellowship with compromised evangelicals are enshrined in the final paragraph of the British Evangelical Council statement
on ecumenicity, which reads, "We wish to affirm,
however, our sincere desire to remain in personal
fellowship with all who are truly Christ's."[35]

The attitude of militant, polemical separatism
seen in C. H. Spurgeon during the 'Downgrade'
controversy, E. J. Poole-Connor in his writings,
and D. M. Lloyd-Jones during the late 1960s in
particular has been subjected to considerable attack
since the death of Dr. Lloyd-Jones on 1st March
1981.

The funeral of Dr. Lloyd-Jones was hardly over
and his imposing figure had scarcely been removed
from this earthly scene when the first voices were
heard stating that they never had really believed
in the necessity of secession.

Soon the cry was being heard that the divisions
of the 1960s were unnecessary and that the unity
of the 1950s which ignored the issue of secession
was desirable. A conference on preaching was called
by a group of Anglican and nonconformist ministers[36] which reviewed the past decades in the following terms, "We regret the sad and often unnecessary
divisions that have marred our unity in recent years"
and expressed the hope that a "spin-off" of the
conference would be "a renewed fellowship and
encouragement of one another in our common
task". The conference was aimed at "younger evangelicals already engaged in regular preaching ministry
within the Anglican and Free Churches".[37]

As the charismatic movement spread through
the churches and created a unity (regardless of
doctrine), the divisions of the 1960s began to be
healed. As common cause was made in Mission
England 1984 the divisions began to be forgotten.
One minister argued for involvement in Mission
England thus, "One difficulty I do not have, and
that is of associating for the sake of the Gospel
with other evangelicals from 'mixed denominations'
such as Anglicans". Later he dismissed those who
hesitated to do this as exclusivist, time-wasting,
in-fighters. The reason why he had no difficulty
in associating with ministers of mixed denominations in the Mission England programme he gave
in one sentence, "I am not associating with them
as Anglicans but as evangelicals".[38] This superb
piece of Nelsonian blindness, whereby he sees what
he wants to see in his associates and ignores the
rest, needs no comment.

1984 also saw the FIEC Council issuing an invitation to an Anglican minister to address its annual assembly — an Anglican minister who is undoubtedly a committed evangelical, and who claims, "I am an evangelical first and an Anglican second."[39] Some of his keenest nonconformist supporters see him as "the best nonconformist the Church of England has" and his church as "effectively an independent evangelical church within the Church of England."[40]

The invitation to an Anglican to address the FIEC Assembly is undoubtedly historic. It is a public declaration by the FIEC that it repudiates the old separatist position because it gives public fellowship to a man who remains in a mixed denomination. It is an essential rejection of the position advocated by E. J. Poole-Connor, Dr. Lloyd-Jones and the British Evangelical Council in the late 1960s.

In a letter written before the FIEC Assembly, Rev. T. O. Jenkins agreed that the FIEC speaker was an Anglican reputed to be "of thorough evangelical faith". But he continued, "He is a continuing member of an organised religion which is compromised to the utmost and is avowedly heading for unity with Rome".[41] "Hitting the nail on the head", Mr. Jenkins argues that the *raison d'être* of the FIEC is its dissatisfaction with compromised churchmanship at national and local level. If the FIEC recognises a mixed church as valid then it has no reason for its existence as a separatist organisation. Indeed its existence is a schismatic action!

The slide that has occurred from the position adopted in the late 1960s has not gone unnoticed and has not been unchallenged. C. H. Spurgeon's

present-day successor at the Metropolitan Tabernacle,
Rev. Dr. P. Masters, published a strident and well-
reasoned argument for separation from non-
evangelicals in 1983 entitled "Separation and
Obedience". In his reasoning concerning compromised evangelicals who remain in mixed denominations, Dr. Masters accepted that in the first place
biblical principles of separation had to be taught.
"There are also many evangelicals who are not
very aware of the extent to which their ministers
and denominations are compromised. We have
the task of helping such believers to see what is
wrong and of sensitively bringing them to face
the issue . . . We must always be anxious to reach,
win and help other believers as they face these
issues."[42]

However, Dr. Masters recognises that some ministers have faced the scriptural call to separate and
have rejected it. He requires separation from them
also. "There is no question that we must separate
from such men in obedience to II Thessalonians 3 . . .
When we speak of separation the point must be
emphasised that we have in mind obdurate men
and women who have rejected the Lord's
command."[43]

Dr. Masters goes beyond C. H. Spurgeon, E. J.
Poole-Connor and Dr. D. M. Lloyd-Jones by totally
rejecting any fellowship with such brethren after
separation has taken place. He repudiates the idea
of maintaining private fellowship whilst rejecting
public formal fellowship. Using II Thessalonians
3 as his basis he argues, "Because the offender is a
professing evangelical we have a duty to do something

in addition to separating — we are to admonish the person. Paul's words do not mean that *officially* we separate but *unofficially* we continue to have friendly relations. They mean that we separate with a serious attempt to warn the offender of the error of his ways."[44]

1983 also saw a separate expression of concern. An *ad hoc* group of ministers met in London[45] and decided that the slide that was being observed from the position of the late 1960s needed to be challenged. They called together a meeting of ministers they believed would be sympathetic to separatist principles. The meeting was addressed by the author and chaired by Rev. H. Jones. It sought to present a biblical basis for separation from non-evangelicals, limited fellowship with compromised evangelicals and the unity of uncompromised evangelicals.

A resumé of the address was sent to some six hundred ministers and a second meeting for those in agreement with the principles was called. This meeting, however, revealed a great deal of confusion and disagreement over the principles of separation and merely heightened concern about the slide of opinion since the late 1960s.

The most contentious of the issues considered was not whether it was correct to separate from non-evangelicals but the nature of the separation from compromised evangelicals that is required by the scriptures. Some advocated no separation, as seen in the late 1950s; others advocated public but not private separation, as seen in the late 1960s; others advocated full separation, as expounded by Dr. Masters. Amongst those committed to "first level separation" (i.e. separation from non-evangelicals) this remains the most contentious issue.

3. Those differences between evangelicals which are not fundamental

In opposing modernism and Catholicism, C. H. Spurgeon saw himself fighting for the fundamentals. Although he was militantly a Calvinist[46] and retained a closed baptised membership at the Metropolitan Tabernacle where he was pastor, he recognised that his fight in the 'Downgrade' was one that non-Calvinist, non-Baptist evangelicals could be involved in also.

He repudiated all suggestions that the 'Downgrade' controversy was over interpretations of the evangelical faith. Rather it was over the acceptance or rejection of the evangelical faith. "In our fellowship with Methodists of all grades we have found them firmly adhering to those great evangelical doctrines for which we contend . . . We care far more for the central evangelical truths than we do for Calvinism as a system . . . Those who hold the eternal verities of salvation and yet do not see all that we believe and embrace are by no means the objects of our opposition: our warfare is with men who are giving up the atoning sacrifice, denying the inspiration of Holy Scripture, and casting slurs upon justification by faith. The present struggle is not a debate on the question of Calvinism or Arminianism, but of the truth of God versus the inventions of men."[47]

The question arises, therefore, as to how C. H. Spurgeon dealt with those of his beliefs which were not common to all evangelicals but which he believed to be biblical. Did he treat them as matters on which evangelicals ought not to divide, as many in the modern world do? The answer to that question is that whereas C. H. Spurgeon stood with and supported those who were evangelicals regardless of their differences with him, and whereas he would be in a formal union with such (e.g. he proposed an evangelical but not a Calvinistic basis for the Baptist Union), in his own preaching and church order he was never less than a Calvinist or a Baptist.

With regard to his Calvinism, Rev. I. Murray has furnished lengthy evidence of C. H. Spurgeon's advocacy of Calvinism and opposition to Arminianism.[48] It was his own boast "We do not conceal our Calvinism in the least".[49] Even when invited to preach among Arminians he preached Calvinism, to their considerable consternation![50] The confessions of faith issued by C. H. Spurgeon, the tone of his sermons, the emphasis in his teaching: all were uncompromisingly Calvinistic.[51]

In the same way, having come to believer's baptism out of a paedo-baptist background, he maintained a closed baptised membership for his church (although an open Lord's table).[52] When someone suggested that C. H. Spurgeon allowed his members to have their infants baptised if they desired it, he reacted strongly, "We do not believe in two baptisms. A man can only be either baptised or buried once. If either of the two baptisms before us is Scriptural the other is unscriptural. We would not have any man, for the sake of a supposed charity, act so inconsistently as to promote two baptisms: let him cleave to the one which he believes to be of the

Lord's ordaining, but let him not flirt with the other. Trifling with conscience and with the laws of God's house has become far too common in these days."[53]

C. H. Spurgeon would have fellowship between churches and believers who differed on these issues. He even appointed a Congregationalist as the chief tutor at his ministerial college.[54] But he did not view those truths, even though they were not among the "eternal verities", as able to be ignored in preaching or practice.

The heirs of C. H. Spurgeon have largely adopted a different view. E. J. Poole-Connor, the FIEC and BEC, Dr. Lloyd-Jones, etc. all viewed Calvinism, baptism and many similar issues as secondary, i.e. not of the essence of evangelicalism. In this C. H. Spurgeon would have agreed. However, they went beyond him in seemingly implying that churches which held firmly to a Calvinistic or Baptistic order were over-emphasising those aspects of the faith. The tendency has developed to view a church which maintains a baptised membership as schismatic, for example. The division between primary and secondary truth has become such a part of modern separatist dogma that any church that wants to be more distinctive than merely evangelical is viewed with suspicion and her desire to stand for real unity amongst evangelicals is open to question.

It is a very unfortunate thing that a willingness to open up the church membership to all types of evangelical belief and practice has become a mark of evangelical separatist orthodoxy. It has created special problems and tensions for Strict Baptists and Presbyterians who both have a greater consciousness

of confessional standards than most other churches.
C. H. Spurgeon's insistence on baptism before
membership of the local church and his militant
Calvinism would be seen as an irritant in the modern
evangelical separatist scene.

The position of C. H. Spurgeon calls us not to
treat those things that divide evangelicals as unimportant or insignificant. Rather it calls us to a
desire for biblical teaching and practice in the local
church (and outside it) with a recognition of those
great truths that unite all evangelicals and a respect
for each other as we follow out our respective interpretations of the scriptures in other areas.

C. H. Spurgeon would not have rejoiced in the
prospect of a local church which had no definite
view of baptism, Calvinism, church government,
the charismatic gifts and prophecy. He expected
preaching to be clear and dogmatic, church life to
be conformed to the understanding God had granted
to the church, respect to be shown to those who
differed yet without compromise of the local
church's belief and position. Perhaps it is time for
us to abandon the prevailing idea that the local
church should be a *"pot-pourri"* and to return to
the idea of local churches holding fast their beliefs
yet respecting the integrity of other evangelical
churches which differ. The all-inclusive evangelical
church of the last few decades can hardly be said
to be a glorious success. It seems rather to have
produced flabby, non-doctrinally minded, confused
congregations.

4. Evangelical unity

C. H. Spurgeon's experience of the ease with which

formal alliances were infiltrated and corrupted
made him very wary of all suggestions that uncompromised evangelicals should be in a formal
union together. In the days leading up to the
battles within the denominations he said, "It is
one thing to overleap all boundaries of denominational restriction for the truth's sake: this we
hope all godly men will do more and more".[55]
Before the battle was lost he hoped for "an
informal alliance among all who hold the Christianity of their fathers".[56]

After C. H. Spurgeon left the Union he expressed
his hopes as follows: "The instinct of the gracious
life is to seek congenial communion, and hence
the necessity of some form of fellowship for ourselves and our churches will suggest itself to those
who sorrowfully come forth from the old camp.
To institute such a thing formally, and ask persons
to join it, would be folly. It must grow up of itself —
by the demand of those who desire it, and then it
will be true and lasting. I do not, therefore, move
in this direction till I hear from other brethren of
like mind that they desire to do so. It will not harm
us to abide alone for a little while, till we see where
we are; and then, whether we are few or many, we
can unite to help our poorer brethren, and to conserve the faith. Our desire is not to oppose others
but that we may strengthen each other's hands in
the Lord. Utterly isolated church life would have
its evils and in true union there will be not only
strength but joy. This will come in due time if it
be the Lord's will."[57]

C. H. Spurgeon saw the way ahead as an informal

alliance of those separatists that desired fellowship. Nothing organised or formal was desired or envisaged. However, he saw such union as not being limited to one strand of evangelical thought. "Denominational divisions sink in the presence of the truth of God. To my mind, the grand distinction to now be observed is found in evangelical doctrine, of which our Lord's substitutionary sacrifice is the centre and soul. Where we see faithful brethren struggling we ought to lay ourselves out to help them . . . Lovers of the old faith should stand shoulder to shoulder."[58]

Where C. H. Spurgeon found meetings arranged by evangelical church groupings exclusively he attended and took part.[59] In the early months of 1890 he banded together with six other brethren to form a fraternal with a basis of faith which was evangelical, Calvinistic, and pre-millenial. The membership was not confined to Baptists and soon grew to about thirty. Together they arranged meetings in defence of the faith, prayed, consulted and studied the scriptures.[60]

These fairly informal ministerial alliances were all that C. H. Spurgeon would commit himself to. He believed the like-minded would work together and stay together without organisations which would so easily corrupt.

The heirs of C. H. Spurgeon have largely put their faith in two types of organisation — the church to church alliance, e.g. FIEC, or the church grouping alliance, e.g. BEC.

Certain criticisms have been raised of these attempts at formal unity. Without strong leadership it is virtually impossible to maintain separatist principles. The main weakness of any church to church alliance that is formalised, is that the group gains an identity all of its own and then finds it easier to defend the actions of its members than to direct or discipline them.

When such groups join together in a group to group alliance there is always the problem of each group trying to maintain its influence and defending its policies rather than seeking the good of the whole.

The informal alliance based on agreed doctrines and a common understanding of the basis of meeting has much more to commend it and probably has more opportunity of success. In May 1984 a statement was sent out by a small group of evangelical ministers[61] to some of their fellow ministers. It sought to set out the negative and positive aspects of separatist principles, calling men to fellowship together on an informal basis. The aim was not to set up an organisation but to encourage like-minded ministers to meet, pray, fellowship, encourage and inform.

Whether the visible unity of uncompromised evangelicals will take steps forward in these coming days is difficult to tell in mid-1984. Unless evangelicals are willing to stand firm for the gospel against its counterfeits and to stand together to this end, the days ahead look bleak indeed. In such times (as always) confidence in God is more powerful than trust in the very best plans of men.

References

1. 'The Sword and Trowel' November 1887 p. 559. For the evidence of the other men and bodies quoted, see chapter nine.
2. Ferm, R. O. (1958). *Co-operative Evangelism: Is Billy Graham Right or Wrong?* Zondervan.
3. Watts, M. (January– March 1984) 'Bible League Quarterly' pp. 204–205.
4. Watts, M. op. cit. p. 205 for details.
5. 'Church of England Newspaper' April 15th 1983. Quoted Watts, M. op. cit. p. 202.
6. MacLeod, D. (1984) Focus Page. 'Monthly Record of the Free Church of Scotland'.
7. 'FIEC News' No. 19 January 1984.
8. Jenkins, T. O. (May/June 1984) Letters to the Editor. 'Fellowship' Magazine.
9. 'The Sword and Trowel' October 1887 p. 510.
10. Baxter, B. E. (1981) *Charismatic Gift of Tongues,* Kregel p. 127.
11. Matterson, E. E. (1968) *The Biblical Faith of Baptists.* The Bryant Press, Vol. 3. p. 119.
12. Brinsmead, R. D. (February 1974) The Current Religious Scene and the Gospel Present Truth.
13. O'Conner, E. (1971) *The Pentecostal Movement in the Catholic Church.* Ave Maria Press p. 191.
14. O'Conner, E. (1970) *Pentecost in the Catholic Church,* Dover Publications pp. 14, 15.
15. Brinsmead, R. D. op. cit. p. 10.
16. 'The Sword and Trowel' August 1887 p. 400.
17. 'The Sword and Trowel' September 1887 pp. 464–5.
18. 'The Sword and Trowel' October 1887 p. 511.
19. ibid. p. 515.
20. ibid. pp. 558–560.
21. Spurgeon, C. H. (1973) Autobiography Vol. II. *The Full Harvest.* Banner of Truth p. 479.
22. 'The Sword and Trowel' January 1888 p. 44.
23. MacLeod, D. op. cit. p. 108.
24. 'The Sword and Trowel:. 1879.
25. 'The Sword and Trowel' October 1888 p. 562.
26. 'The Sword and Trowel' December 1888 pp. 617–620.
27. 'The Sword and Trowel' 1889 pp. 578–579, 624.
28. 'The Sword and Trowel' 1890 pp. 93, 94, 392, 393, 460.
29. 'The Sword and Trowel' 1891 pp. 149, 249, 348, 349.
30. 'The Life of Faith' Thursday 25th January 1968, p. 1.
31. Rev. J. Stott.

32. Rev. J. I. Packer was excluded from the Committee. Anglicans, however, may attend (contra. D. MacLeod op. cit. p. 180).
33. Masters, P. M. (1983) Separation and Obedience p. 2.
34. Lloyd-Jones, D. M. (1968) *Luther and His Message for Today.* Evangelical Press.
35. BEC Policy Statement on Ecumenicity.
36. Revs. J. Barrs, S. Bickley, R. Clements, A. Green, J. Hodder, R. Lucas, D. Jackman, R. Macaulay, K. Stokes.
37. Invitation letter to "The Word at Work Conference".
38. Middleton, D. (March/April 1984) Mission England. 'Fellowship' Magazine p. 9.
39. Lucas, R. (March/April 1984) Interview. 'Fellowship' Magazine. p. 16.
40. Comments of Rev. Leith Samuel, former minister of Above Bar Church, Southampton.
41. Jenkins, T. O. op. cit.
42. Masters, P. M. op. cit. p. 7.
43. ibid. p. 8.
44. ibid. p. 8.
45. Revs. E. Alldritt, W. Lyall, R. Cotton, H. Waite, D. Webber, T. O. Jenkins, H. Jones, R. Sheehan.
46. See Murray, I. (1966) *The Forgotten Spurgeon.* Banner of Truth pp. 53–120.
47. 'The Sword and Trowel' April 1887 pp. 195–196. See also p. 642.
48. See Murray, I. op. cit. pp. 53–120.
49. 'The Sword and Trowel' December 1887 p. 642.
50. Spurgeon, C. H. (1965) *Twelve Sermons on Holiness,* Reiner Publications pp. 15–16.
51. Spurgeon, C. H. (1973) *The Early Years.* Banner of Truth, Chapter 13.
52. ibid. pp. 119, 145–52.
53. 'The Sword and Trowel' December 1889 p. 530.
54. Spurgeon, C. H. Autobiography Vol. II. *The Full Harvest.* Banner of Truth. p. 446.
55. 'The Sword and Trowel' August 1887 p. 400.
56. ibid. p. 400.
57. 'The Sword and Trowel' June 1888 p. 299.
58. 'The Sword and Trowel' July 1888 p. 344.
59. 'The Sword and Trowel' July 1889 pp. 389, 390. August 1889 p. 456.
60. 'The Sword and Trowel' August 1891 pp. 446–448.
61. Revs. E. Alldritt, R. Cotton, H. Jones, W. Lyall, R. Lamb, R. Sheehan, T. O. Jenkins, H. Waite, D. Webber.